Ishwar

Modern Indian Architecture

Ishwar

Modern Indian Architecture

ISBN/EAN: 9783337385156

Printed in Europe, USA, Canada, Australia, Japan

Cover: Foto ©Thomas Meinert / pixelio.de

More available books at **www.hansebooks.com**

Modern Indian Architecture,

Adapted to the use of Artisans, Students, Builders, and Architects.

(WITH THIRTY-TWO PLATES.)

BY

ISHWAR.

"*Practical wisdom acts in the mind as gravitation does in the material world, combining, keeping things in their places, and maintaining a mutual dependence amongst the various parts of our system. It is for ever reminding us where we are, and what we can do, not in fancy, but in real life.*"—Sir Arthur Helps.

BOMBAY:
PRINTED AT THE
EDUCATION SOCIETY'S STEAM PRESS.

1892.

Colonel W. S. S. BISSET, C.I.E., R.E.,

Agent, B. B. & C. I. Railway, including Rajputana-Malwa Railway.

SIR,

I regard your kind permission to dedicate this my work to you both a pleasure and a privilege, and it affords me the opportunity of acknowledging many acts of kindness received at your hands.

Your encouragement of whatever is conducive to general utility, gives me hope that, however humble the merits of this work may be, you will approve my desire to add my quota to the stock of knowledge available to the Public on the important Practical Business of the Engineer and Architect.

I have the honor to be,

Sir,

Your most obedient servant,

TUKARAM.

TABLE OF CONTENTS.

INTRODUCTION.

Architecture may certainly be classed as one of the Fine Arts, more especially when the term is used to distinguish the difference between Designing and Building. Architecture has somewhere been defined as *building according to rule*, but a better interpretation would perhaps be *building artistically*. The beauty and elegance of a building, due to the architectural correctness of its proportions, demonstrate the art of the designer, and can be appreciated by the uneducated as well as by those who are conversant with the principles of construction. All living creatures build houses and may be said to have a knowledge of building; but man ornaments his structures, and builds them with a view to please the eye of his fellow creatures, and with a desire to appeal to their mental susceptibilities: it is knowledge of architecture as an art that enables him to do this.

In India are found buildings, both ancient and modern, of orders or types of architecture very different from what is seen in European cities. Many of the temples, palaces, &c., are of exceeding beauty, and the delicacy and intricacy of detail to be found in them cannot be surpassed in any other country in the world. Great strength and stability are also prominent in many of the various types of architecture to be met with in the extensive country known as India.

India is renowned for being able to supply, not only some of the best workmen in the world, but is also rich in material of all kinds required for building: stone, timber, and many of the metals being in abundance. As instances of both design and workmanship, we may mention the *Taj Mahal* and Emperor Akbar's Mausoleum or *Sicandra* at Agra, the *Durgha*, *Shaik Salem Chishti* at Futtehpore Sikri, the *Jumma Musjid* and *Kutub Minar* at Delhi, and the Golden Temple at Armitsar. Also the Cave Temples in the Deccan, the Temple of Jaggunnath at Puri, in Orissa, and many others in all parts of this vast country.

The exquisite beauty of many of the ancient examples of Indian architecture has always attracted, and still continues to attract, lovers of Art from all parts of the world. Painters, sculptors and others come to gaze and wonder at the greatness of the intellect that designed the structures, and at the marvellous care and patience that must have been expended in carrying out the designs.

Indian architecture may be said broadly to be of two quite distinct types, *viz.*, Hindoo and Mahomedan. The Hindoo type is of course the oldest; and, as some of the earliest examples of it, may be named the Ruins of Mansions at Khujram in Central India, the Cave Temples in the Deccan, and the Temples of Maharaja Prithvi Raj at Delhi and Ajmere.

The Mahomedan type is of several distinct classes. Buildings of the time of the Pathan dynasty being marked by massive and gigantic proportions, while buildings erected in the time of the Emperors Akbar and Jehangir were of a very elegant and artistic style, thereby showing that rapid strides had been made in the art of erecting buildings that would please the eye and mind. Some of the best specimens of what might be called the middle Mahomedan style are the Mausoleum of the Emperor Akbar at Agra, the Sheik Salem Chishti's Durga at Futtehpore Sikri, and the Mahals in the Fort at Agra. A third, and even more beautiful style of architecture, was introduced during the time of the Emperor Shah Jehan, and during his dynasty more buildings of surpassing beauty and elegance of design were erected than during any other period; nothing equal to them in chasteness and richness of design had ever been seen before, and it may be doubted if the world elsewhere can shew anything to compare with them. The cities of Delhi, Agra, Muttra, Jeypore and Ulwar abound with specimens of this last-mentioned type, and one never tires of gazing on the beauty of them.

It is much to be regretted that in this present age the study of Indian architecture is almost entirely neglected, the design and erection of buildings being now in the hands of those who have no special knowledge of the Art, other than as builders or workers in material, such as masons, carpenters,

&c. This is much to be regretted, and is no doubt largely due to the fact that there are but few books on the subject which would enable the builder and artizan to attain a knowledge of the principles to be followed in designing a building, which shall be not only useful but ornamental, and in harmony with surroundings.

Architecture, like other Arts and Sciences, is based on fixed principles and formulæ, an acquaintance with which is absolutely necessary as a commencement to those who desire to pursue its study technically; and, with this object in view, the author has prepared drawings shewing details of the scientific and mechanical proportions of the different styles. These drawings are presented to the public accompanied by a full description of each plate, giving the proportions and technical names of the different parts, &c. In order to create a familiarity with Hïndustani technical terms, these have been used in their own vernacular; but a compendious glossary at the end of the work furnishes English equivalents for the same, or supplies the explanation necessary for a complete understanding of them.

In the opening chapter will be found some general remarks on Architecture. This is followed by another chapter containing a description of the general principles which should be followed, when designing a building, in order that the structure, when complete, shall satisfy the eye with its beauty, and the understanding with its strength.

GENERAL REMARKS.

Man cultivates many arts; some that are strictly utilitarian; some contributing to the increase of luxury, and others combining in themselves both utility and luxury. Architecture, comprehensively viewed, may be classed as one of the arts which not only supplies our natural wants and assists our natural infirmities, but also secures, preserves, accommodates, delights, gratifies, flatters, and gives consequence to the human race. Of it, it can safely be asserted, that it plays no inconsiderable part in almost every comfort or luxury of life; and few would be so daring as to regard it as a means for the promotion of luxury only.

The first advances in civilization taught the savage to provide for the greater comfort of the body, and thereby of the mind also, by the erection of huts, or the occupation of caves and other sheltered places. Exposed, as he must have been, to the inclemencies of the weather, we can imagine what a struggle must have taken place in the mind of the human being in his native state of barbarism, before he decided on isolating himself under such protection as he could manufacture or avail himself of, or continue a victim to the uncertainties of the seasons. Gregarious by nature, this separation from the society of his fellows must at first have been irksome. But it was the breaking of the first link in the fetters of barbarism: and the accompanying comforts and luxuries of faculties no longer benumbed; an atmosphere more temperate amid heat and cold; capability to sleep when desired at ease and in security, and dispositions neither indolent in summer nor dull and abject in winter, must have rapidly caused the remaining links to be burst asunder. The isolated cave or hut soon developed into a settlement, and more commodious dwellings (by force of association if by nothing else) gradually disclosed a purer taste for the sweets of social enjoyments. With a body more vigorous, a spirit more active, ingenious and enterprising, and a mind more speculative, agriculture and arts commenced, improved and flourished; and the erewhile denizen of the forests, who at one time knew no other covering but his leafy shades, learned to provide himself, at first with the necessaries, then with the conveniences, and next with the luxuries of this life. It is in this manner that Architecture claims for itself an important factorship in the advance of civilization. But the progress still continued. Inventions followed, and facilitated man's efforts; labour became shortened, and productions increased; domestic wants were satisfied, and provision made for the future; while Nature's bountifulness, still unstinted, gave to Architecture the credit of smoothing the way for the beginning of commerce. The taste of wealth, and the desire for more, or perhaps the gratification of his natural inclination to conquer and overcome, taught man to form roads through marshes or other ground impracticable by nature; to fill up valleys; to unite or level mountains; to throw bridges over deep and rapid waters; to turn aside or lessen the fury of torrents; to construct navigable canals; to build ships; and to construct harbours and seaports. The source of wealth having been discovered, a thousand superfluous and artificial cravings now sprang into existence, most of which could not be gratified without the aid of architecture. These were splendid palaces, magnificent temples, costly dwelling houses, theatres and amphitheatres, baths and porticos, triumphal arches, mausoleums, and every conceivable accessory to ease, pleasure, wealth, grandeur, and pre-eminence.

Architecture differs from other objects in being more certainly productive of design, more permanent in effect, and more beneficial in its consequence. The other usual appendages of wealth, such as furniture, dress, equipages, and large retinues, are at first only secondary attractions. Their value changes or dies with the hour: they all feel the effect of time. The productions of Architecture command universal attention, survive the decaying influences of time, and descend to posterity.

More immediately, Architecture offers great benefits to the world at large by the employment of numerous labourers, workmen, and artificers; by converting materials of little value into the most stately productions of human skill; and by beautifying the face of Nature. It is also by means of Architecture that generations yet to come learn of the virtues, achievements, and munificence of their ancestors in past ages. In it many arts and manufactures are required to furnish and adorn buildings, consequently Architecture may be said with all truth to occupy thousands and constitute many lucrative branches of commerce. Cities renowned for their buildings attract a large concourse of strangers and visitors, who extend its fame, adopt its fashions, give it reputation, and create a demand for its productions. To this day the stately structures of ancient Delhi, Agra, and other parts of India largely contribute to the splendours of the present by the number of travellers who flock from all nations to visit their edifices; to purchase their curiosities and art productions, and even to take up their residence in these historical cities. Thus it may be accurately asserted that Architecture contributes to modern magnificence by the vast sums of money it keeps to bring to the cities in which its unique specimens abound, and over which the lapse of even seven centuries is scarcely perceivable.

Nor is Architecture less useful in defending countries. It secures boundaries, fortifies cities, controls the ambition, frustrates the attempts of foreign powers, curbs their insolence, and averts the dangers and horrors of war.

As shewn above, Architecture procures for the body both health and vigour, facilitates inventions, promotes commerce, and points the way for men to employ their riches rationally, nobly, and benevolently, in a manner equally useful to themselves and their descendants. It adds splendour to the State, shows us how to defend our possessions, and protects mankind from attempts of lawless violence or unrestrained ambition.

No wonder then that an art conducive of so many advantages to the happiness and prosperity of nations, has always commanded protection and encouragement. In all civilized times and well-regulated governments has Architecture been liberally attended to and promoted with unremitting assiduity. As a natural consequence, its own promotion has been accompanied by the furtherance of other arts; as for example, the sister arts of painting and sculpture, and all the inferior branches of decorative workmanship. To a commercial people this is of the highest importance. For, where these arts flourish, they must have an influence on manufactures. Even the minutest mechanical productions, the slightest variety of design or increase of skill, commands additional remuneration, and the subject can need no further illustration.

We must not, however, suppose that the mere heaping of stone upon stone and calling it Architecture can produce the results already detailed, or reflect honour either on nations or individuals. Writers on the art of building have compared the materials used in Architecture to words in phraseology. Both have separately only little power; both may be so arranged as to create ridicule, disgust, or even contempt, or to move the mind to admiration. It is apparent then that the necessary qualification to the beneficial use of either is skill, and not skill only, but skill expressed with energy. Rustic language may be so handled by the able writer as to dignify itself; while the weak efforts of the ignorant may be so wretchedly disposed as to destroy the costliest enrichments.

Architecture is generally divided into three great classes, *viz.*—military, naval, and civil. It will be allowed that the last is of the most general use; and to it I purpose to confine myself in the present work, not only on account of its broader scope, but also because it is the branch to which my own study and practice have been more immediately applied.

After having remained for so many years in obscurity it must not be supposed that so difficult an art as Architecture should at once emerge into full perfection. With very little assistance from books, and that for the most part obscure, unintelligible, and erroneous, the first restorers of the ancient manner of building could not at once bring it to a degree of purity, incapable of further improvement. They had to contend against length of time, casualties, and even war. While they laboured to separate beauty from deformity under such heavy disadvantages, they left much undone and taught many errors. Reverencing the memory of these illustrious artists, we must neither censure their omissions, nor wonder at their mistakes. We have to remember that their measures and designs were, generally speaking, incorrect, that their plates were ill-engraved, and that their want of method in treating their subjects, renders the study of it in their works exceedingly discouraging. More recent authors have, however, supplied these omissions and rectified these faults: and in the present day there are few subjects that have been more amply treated than Architecture, nor any by persons better qualified, in so much that little remains either to be discovered or improved. Every branch of the art has been maturely considered and made as certain as it is capable of being so. The one thing that remained to be done was to collect into one volume what lay dispersed in many, or what was written in a foreign language, or, worse still, known only to artificers and irresponsible persons.

It will be readily conceded by the student of Architecture that there are few pursuits more perplexing because the connections which constitute truth or fallacy are often far distant and beyond the ken of superficial observers. The vague foundation on which the more refined parts of the art are built, has given rise to a multiplicity of conflicting opinions, one and all supported by plausible arguments. The task of discriminating and distinguishing what is real from what is specious is, therefore, one of considerable difficulty. The merit of performances is too often measured by the fame of the performer, by the test of the age in which they were produced, by vulgar report, by party opinion, or by some other standard equally inadequate; and not seldom, by precepts delivered centuries ago, and calculated for other climates, other men, and other customs.

It is the removal of these drawbacks and inconveniences that the author had in view when he ventured to attempt the present work. Its objects are greatly to shorten the labours of the student and to lead him to the truth by easier and more inviting paths; to make the study of Architecture and its attendant arts more general; to promote true taste, and to diffuse the love of what is really excellent in the curiosities of antiquity among those who are the fit encouragers of elegance, *viz.*, persons of high rank and large fortune. His design was without national bias or other prejudice to consider what had been produced upon the subject, and to collect from the writings of others, or from his own observation in many parts of India, whatever particulars seemed most interesting, to furnish a correct idea of so very useful and truly noble an art as Architecture is. Aware that bad or indifferent artists have been produced in all ages, and that all men are liable to error, no matter how excellent they may be, it has been his intention neither to be influenced by particular times, nor by the general reputation of particular persons. In cases where reason or demonstration could be used, he has employed them; and where they could not, he has substituted generally admitted opinion. Abstruse or fruitless arguments are avoided, and readers not much acquainted with Architecture are not perplexed with a number of indiscriminate examples. In fact, it has been judged more expedient to present only a few, and of the kind calculated to serve both as standards for imitation and guides. Care has been taken to be precise, perspicuous, and brief in the language employed; and the designs have been selected as examples of simplicity, richness, order, character, and beauty of form. The necessary qualifications and duty in these modern days of the architect are briefly explained; and in the course of the work, many additional hints, explanations, and elucidations have been inserted wherever they seemed necessary. It has been attempted, on different occasions, to point out to the beginner and student the course he ought to follow, the dangers he has to shun, and the object he must continually keep in view. So constant have been the writer's avocations, that in the course of twenty years it has never been properly in his power to set about this undertaking; and a variety of concurring circumstances render it less so now than ever. Loose materials have indeed been abundantly collected, and many designs have from time to time been made, with an eye to the general intention; but there are so many more to make, correct, or methodize, that the author must reluctantly relinquish the remainder to some other pen. What has not been treated of, though perhaps important to builders, is of no consequence to connoisseurs or men of taste, who aspire to be judges of the beauties or deformities of structures.

THE ELEMENTS OF BEAUTY IN ARCHITECTURE.

There is perhaps no subject on which differences of opinion are more apt to arise than on the beauty or otherwise of a building. Nor should this statement prove astonishing. For, when we consider that the bases of designs vary greatly in the different styles, and are limited only by the range of animate and inanimate creation, it will, I think, be manifest that, in an art which has no regulated standard of comparison, opinions must often be at variance. In Architecture the creative power of nature herself is the model imitated. It is an art that appeals directly to the understanding, and it does not attract the senses in the same way as the sister arts of painting and music. For this reason the productions of the architect are not so universally appreciated as those of the painter and musician, and, in fact, are understood only by those whose judgment is trained by education. The beautiful models of nature are the index and guide of the painter and sculptor, and a successful imitation of these models is capable of affecting us with very agreeable sensations. Other arts readily address the senses and passions, but the architect relies only on his appeal to the understanding. An architect's power of attraction is therefore limited to operations on the cultivated mind. By the untrained, magnitude and richness are more valued than elegance of form or the most fascinating arrangement of proportions. The artist's object is not so much to investigate metaphysically the wherefore of the beauty in the productions of his art, as to study the effects that follow from the carrying out of those principles which, by the common consent of ages, are esteemed beautiful. It is in this way that an artist will more readily obtain information regarding those qualities, universally known as beauty, which act on the understanding, and at the same time excite our affections. These qualities may be arranged into three classes, in accordance with the actions they produce, *viz.*: (1) qualities which affect the eye; (2) qualities which affect the understanding; (3) qualities which excite the senses or passions, and in which taste is the principal guide. To denominate these three classes in a simpler manner I will correspondingly call them :—

(1) Magnitude and strength.

(2) Order and harmony.

(3) Richness and simplicity.

These qualities answer to the three great divisions of the subject which have been adopted by writers on Architecture, *viz.*, *Construction*, in which the chief requisites are magnitude and strength; *Design and Disposition*, in which the principal requisites are order and harmony; and *Decoration*, the requisites of which are richness or simplicity, according to the nature of the composition.

There are, however, many other circumstances which tend to the production of an agreeable and beautiful result. One of these may be more particularly noticed, as there can be no doubt of its influence in causing our admiration of the splendid buildings of India, and that is, association with the times and countries most hallowed in our imagination. It is difficult to look at ancient buildings without being carried back in our minds to the times of the polished nations who were the designers and erectors of them. This association with other times and countries is one of the causes that must produce on the mind of at least every man of taste, that feeling which readily assigns to the contemplated structures, a very extraordinary and exalted degree of beauty.

Magnitude and Strength.—We are assured from experience that, beyond certain limits, size and strength, when alone displayed in Architecture, cease to be beautiful. In fact, beyond a given limit, any mass of matter which fatigues the eye by the effort expended in the more than ordinary dimensions is not by any means an agreeable object. In Architecture excessive magnitude may be considered an illegitimate appeal to the senses. To illustrate what is meant I would mention the instance of a gallery of such length that the eye cannot with distinctness penetrate to the end; or, of a column too lofty; or, of a building whose site is such that the visual angle can never include its extent; or, of a building too much elevated under the same circumstances. In short, all excessive dimensions are as distressing to the eye as a light which is too strong. Going to the other extreme, there is repugnance to objects in Architecture which are extremely diminutive. In these the eye is limited and constrained within such narrow bounds, that it experiences almost the same sensations as are imparted when endeavouring to read by the flame of an inefficient light.

Writers on the principles of taste have made magnitude a quality necessary to the existence of the sublime. That it is so in works of nature, associated with ideas of power, danger, and terror, is undeniable; but it will scarcely be admitted that these ideas can be said to find a place in the productions of Architecture, and magnitude may, in them, perhaps, be properly classed among the essentials of beauty.

It would be difficult to conceive that any work in the art under our examination could be considered beautiful if unaccompanied by requisite strength or stability, or at least such an appearance of either as would carry a conviction to the mind that it possessed a sufficiency of these properties for its existence and duration. Though magnitude, speaking widely, is intimately associated with the idea of proportionable power or strength; yet stability is not necessarily dependent on magnitude.

Strength and stability in Architecture are almost synonymous with fitness or adequacy (in appearance at least) of the several parts of the structure to the due performance of their different offices. Thus strength and stability of structure depend on the fitness of the parts to support themselves and to do the work required of them.

Order and Harmony.—I will now proceed to the consideration of order and harmony as elements of beauty in Architecture. By the word order is meant a disposing of the several parts of a building in their appropriate places in relation to each other and to the whole. Whilst harmony is that which, from its Greek derivation, it would strictly import, *vis.*, a joining together of the parts in a consistent and uniform manner, so that all matter which is foreign or unsuit-able to the composition be rejected.

There are no edifices in any style of Architecture in which harmony is more predominant than in buildings erected in the time of the Emperor Shah Jehan. Harmony may, however, be carried to such an extent as to be monotonous. This is the case in certain types of Indian architecture, in which an excess of repetition as well as an absence of variety cloys without satisfying. Such a type may be compared to a musical composition, strictly conformable to the laws of counterpoint, wherein the author so constantly dwells on the same key that he fails to fix the hearer's attention for more than a few seconds. Harmony can never exist in a building, the subdivisions of which are contrived without such an attention to uniformity of character as to impress on the mind an idea of unity, and, if one may be permitted to use the term, an expression of the structure's purpose. It is, moreover, strictly to be attended to in regulating and modifying the decorations employed. For instance, delicacy, lightness, and richness of ornament would ill suit a building, the character and purpose of which were of a nature dissimilar with those qualities.

Richness and Simplicity. These are qualities, in the discreet use of which Indian architects of the best ages excelled and carried artistically to the highest degree of perfection.

As richness and simplicity belong exclusively to the third division of the art of building, viz., decoration, it follows that ornaments are to be chosen or rejected according to the association which exists between their adoption and the effects which they are calculated to produce on the mind. When an effect of grandeur and stability is aimed at, but few ornaments are admissible, because, many subdivisions of detail, which is the case where decoration is unsparingly used, destroy ideas of strength as they weaken, or appear to weaken, the parts on which they are employed. Hence, according to the purpose of a work should ornamentation and variety thereon be introduced into it, always bearing in mind that excess and overloading with ornament distract and fatigue the eye, and tend to destroy the effect of the best arranged designs.

Decoration, when judiciously introduced, becomes in many instances a language, intelligible only, however, when the artist and spectator are conversant with the rules or grammar of the language. It is then a system of hieroglyphic writing, and the building to which it is applied becomes historical, and tells its tale more nobly and appropriately than it can ever do through the undignified medium of mural inscriptions.

It may not be considered superfluous to draw the attention of the aspiring young architect to the following axiom:—A young man desirous of becoming an architect must first consult the best books at his disposal, as these are the school from which he must collect the rudiments of his profession. Then by practice, experience, and attentive observation, the rest may be attained, and he may become a skilled master of the art.

The architect's aim, as has been previously observed, should be to erect handsome, strong, healthy, and well-arranged buildings; to estimate the cost of constructing the same; and to see that they are fabricated properly and without excessive expenditure. The principles of the art may, therefore, be ranged under four distinct heads—Distribution, Construction, Decoration, and Economy.

Of Construction and Decoration it has already been shown whence his knowledge should be collected; and of Distribution, which comprehends all particulars relative to health, convenience, comfort, pleasure, and profit, the artist may collect his general ideas from books or observations made upon buildings erected for various purposes in different climates and at different times. But it is only by practice in discovering the advantages or defects of situation; the nature of climates or aspects; the qualities of air, water, soil, and many other things necessary to be known that the Architectural student can become expert. And, it is only by a thorough acquaintance with the customs and modes of living of his own times, and with the dispositions, amusements, occupations, and duties of his contemporaries, that he can effectually learn how to supply their wants or gratify their wishes.

In countries where general custom governs most things, and where all persons of the same rank think, act, and live nearly after the same manner, the ny difficulties. But

reat field for investig

mplicated and extensi

uires a perfect know

be treated with a gre

riter has fixed his a

m to limit his resear

different quarries,

ular country or city

eeeed to make himsel

much time and what material are requisite to produce given quantities thereof; what profits according to the usages of the place are allowed thereon to the master-workmen; and in what manner it is measured or accounted for when done, so that he may be entire master of his subject and be able to judge equitably between the employer and employed as his station requires. These enquiries will at first be attended with considerable difficulty for reasons already mentioned. But, like propositions in geometry, one information will facilitate another, and in the course of a few years' practice, the artist, if he be industrious and apt at receiving impressions, will have acquired a thorough knowledge of whatever concerns his own circle.

PLATE I.

[illegible] and Pillars.

The five different columns in this plate came into use after Jehangir's reign. The technical name of the first column is *[illegible]*, and it is used for buildings of every description. This kind of pillar is very beautiful in appearance, but on account of its delicacy it is generally made of stone, as it is not durable in plaster. Where the dimensions of the walls are of great breadth double pillars are used. Below is a list of the technical names of the different parts or members of the column:—

Base—*Tho, mutan, gutia, khumbh.*

Capital—*Tho, gutia, khumbh.*

2nd column.—*Raja Shahi.* This column is so named on account of its being used chiefly by the Hindoos. With the exception of its capital (*khumbh*) and its base (*khumbh*), it entirely consists of *mutan* work.

3rd column.—*Firangana.*—This column owes its name to the circumstance of its having been adopted from the English style of architecture. It can be readily used both for stone and plaster. Its waving scroll work (*[illegible]*) is very beautiful.

4th column.—*Jehangir Shahi.* So called on account of its being in vogue during the reign of Jehangir, the style being extensively adopted during his time and afterwards. This column is plain but very beautiful. The [illegible] in the capital looks very elegant. On the four sides of the *tho* or base it has small *mahrabs* carved in stone.

5th column.—*Sandum.* So called owing to its width being greater than its breadth, the same as with a box. This also looks very beautiful. It is more largely used both in stone and in plaster work. The style is plain and chiefly used in buildings which have thick walls. Specimens of two kinds are given in the plate. A half or part of a pillar, the back of which is built into the wall of a building is called an *aleen*. There are two *aleens* and two pillars in one *sidara*. The following figures shew the comparison between the different proportions of the five columns:—

Name of Column.	Height of Base or Chowki.	Height of Shaft or Dundi.	Height of Capital or Bhunna.	Total Height.	Breadth of Base.
Khumba	3⅝	3⅜	2	9	1½
Raja Shahi................................	1¼	7⅛	1¼	9⅝	1½
Fringana	1½	8¼	1¼	11	2
Jehangier Shahi................................	1¼	7⅝	1⅛	10	2
Sundooki	1¼	7⅜	1⅜	10	2

It will be observed in Plate I. that the different technical names of the parts of the arch are given. Such arches are called *Bungri-dar-makrab*, and are more generally used in all sorts of buildings than other arches are. When cut from a single block of stone they appear especially beautiful. This arch resembles a horse-shoe in shape, and is drawn in the following manner. Take ⅛th of the diameter of the arch and put it below the versed sine, consider that point as centre, describe a circle, and divide half of the arch as follows—It is required to make five *bungri*. Divide the half arch in 7⅜ equal parts. Each *bungri* should be made of one part, the *nag* of 1¾, and the half *chukka* of ⅝ths of a part. Allow for the breadth in the same manner 10 *bux* or equal parts, and for the height 17 *bux* or equal parts as far as the *tanta*. The *chai* meets the *tanta* in the same plane according to the breadth of the base; the thickness of the *chais* and *katuf* together is equal to that of the architrave. The thickness of the *katuf* is less, and serves the purpose of a horizontal bracket, being meant to support the *sardal* or architrave. The *chai* in this place is attached separately, the reason for the separation being that, when economy is wished for, the *katuf* is made less thick, and when the whole is made in one block they are sunk in the block.

PLATE 11.

The Shimer Gola Arch.

These arches are specialities of the [illegible] style, and are used chiefly for large single openings and in [illegible]. They are generally made where the arches are high and broad. These arches also resemble a horse-shoe, and are drawn in the following manner:—Add to the versed sine 1/6th part of the diameter, and from the centre thus found describe a circle. Make 6 equal parts of the height or versed sine, and in 4/6 parts of height and with 5/6 of breadth as major axis, describe an ellipse over the upper part of the arch, and in the remaining portion 2/6 one should be taken as a radius and a ¼ circle described on both sides. The breadth of the arch should be 10 feet and the height 8 feet. But this is not a fixed rule as much depends upon the nature and circumstances of the building. The plinth should be of one step and the *khutamba*, *pawanda*, and *kala* of this arch are generally of stone. If single pillars are fixed it will be a quadrant otherwise [illegible] in pairs can be made. Panels are made in the spandrils of the arch the decorations of which can be of various styles. *Kalyan* also known as *kanri*, are sometimes employed, and [illegible] in the *padam*, but simple lines are as often used.

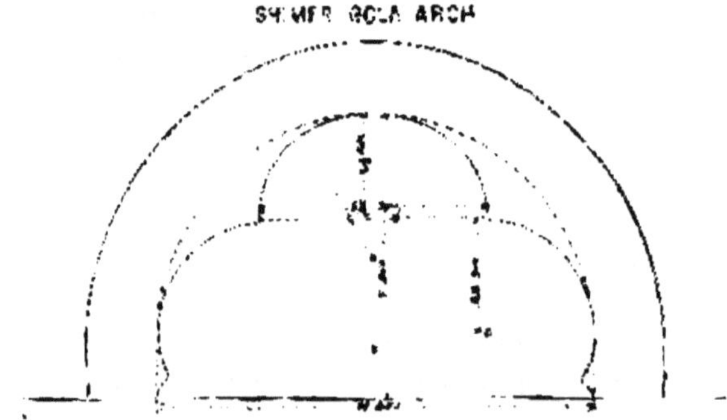

PLATE III.

The Jahangiri Sidra.

This *sidra* came into existence in the time of Jahangir. The thickness of the shaft of this pillar bears the same ratio to its height as 1 to 9½. It has no arches. The lintels are supported over the horizontal brackets and covered by the *chai* at the levels of the capitals in the same plane. In this plate the columns shown are of a very simple style, but they are frequently most elaborately inlaid with all kinds of coloured stones, examples of which will be found in Jahangir's *mahal* at Agra Fort. The best ratio of height to breadth of opening is 1 to 2½; but this rule is not absolute. It depends on circumstances. The plinth should be of one step, and the *khakandas, phrenda*, and *dasa* should be fitted proportionately. The shaft of this column is generally made in the figure of a dodecagon. *Galibs* look very nice in the capitals or *bhunna.* The top is squared so as to get the upper works at right angles to each other.

PLATE IV.

The Fringana.

This style of arch received its name because it was introduced during the British period. The outline of the arch has been copied from European models. This arch is of an oval shape and looks well in the facade of a large building. The pillars or *payas* are of Indian style, are common, and require *pashani* and panels to be elegant. These panels are sunk and the *ijara* raised. The *kursi* or plinth is generally of one step or more as necessity requires. In the plinth *khakandas, phrenda*, and *dasa* are constructed as may be required in proportion to the height of the plinth. Its *pashani* are always double.

PLATE V.

Entrance, Temple, Jahangir.

[illegible] arch was copied from ancient buildings, and has been [illegible] from the [illegible] Jahangir [illegible] has [illegible] frequently been regarded as one [illegible] the [illegible] of the [illegible] during [illegible]. The entrance [illegible] is [illegible]. The [illegible] of several sorts. This shows that the art of [illegible] work, as shown in other plates, was [illegible]. The building from which the plate has been drawn looks very elegant. The [illegible] different [illegible]. The proportions are:

Long [illegible] 9 Haths
Chokra [illegible] $2\frac{1}{2}$
[illegible] [illegible] $5\frac{1}{2}$

The *panam* [illegible] the entrance on all its three sides, and the [illegible] is [illegible] distinctly [illegible].

PLATE VI.

Principal Entrance, Mahomedan Style.

[illegible] is [illegible] to the principal [illegible] of the Taj Mahal at Agra. It is very [illegible] divided into proportions, and its decorations are simple. The [illegible] as a whole, is most graceful. In the [illegible] of the arch *galib* are made, the details of which will be found in the Plate XXIV. Inscriptions in inlaid work will be generally found in the [illegible]. The [illegible] are mostly decorated with [illegible] (*Sati*) or inlaid work, and the [illegible] *[illegible]* [illegible] *[illegible]* are [illegible] in the [illegible] Plate XIX. The *panam* is [illegible] with [illegible], and above these the small openings and little domes, which add greatly to its beauty. These are called *jhomkis*. This entrance is made in octagonal shape, the two sides of the octagon being constructed into a double storey. The octagonal form is prepared for the reason that if it were made in one straight line, it would look very heavy. This kind of pointed arch was introduced into India by the Mahomedans: no specimens being found to exist before their advent. In fact, arch work of any kind is not found in India before the Mahomedan era. In his handbook Mr. H. G. Keene tells us that the Taj was built by Italians. I do not know how far this is correct; but it is certain that the men who built the Taj, also built the palace and the Jamma Musjid at Delhi. The names of these illustrious architects are Usta Hamed and Usta Heera of Narnol, near Delhi, one of them a mason and the other a sculptor. Their names still live in the designations given to two lanes in the vicinity of the famous Jamma Musjid. It would not be right to assert that before the erection of the Taj similar buildings did not exist in India; because Humayun's tomb, a very perfect type of this kind of structure, was built near Delhi about one hundred years previous to the time of Shah Jahan, and it would appear that the design of the Taj was taken from this edifice. The most casual comparison of these two buildings would substantiate the correctness of this statement.

Construction.

The breadth of the large opening is 4½ *bux* and the height 6⅔ *bux*. The height of the entrance below the *pashani* is 7 *bux*, and below the *kungoras* 8 *bux*. The height of the *kungoras* is ⅔ *bux*, and that of the small arch below the *jhomk* 1⅓ *bux*. The breadth of the inner opening is 2 *bux*, the height up to the springing 3⅓ *bux*, and the total height 4½ *bux*. The *pashani* commences above the *ijara*, which is made to project above the plinth, generally to the height of 3 or 3½ feet.

PLATE VII.

[illegible]—[illegible] Entrance.

This kind of principal entrance is [illegible]. Its details are decorated with rising and undulating flower-work. Gables are made over the width of the entrance. The shape of the entrance [illegible] with the [illegible] windows. The network of bands over [illegible] the pattern and the [illegible] on the [illegible] of this network are carved. [illegible] are made on top of its corners, and the balcony above the window stands over the brackets. In the space between the two brackets [illegible] are made, and [illegible] and railings stand over the balcony. These railings are generally half a yard in height, and [illegible] the first storey.

In the second storey [illegible] are ornamented with flowing leaves or [illegible] and on both sides of the entrances [illegible] with [illegible] of [illegible] shape are placed, finishing off with [illegible] at the head.

The height and breadth of the first storey of the entrance are at a ratio of [illegible] to 4, and the breadth and length of the middle portion at a ratio of 3 to 10. The centre spacing is intended to be used for purposes of ingress and egress, while the [illegible] windows on either side are for the use of [illegible]. The height of the [illegible] in the storey above should be two-thirds of that of the first storey. It is inferred from the experience of buildings that the height of upper stories should always be less than that of the lower stories, a proceeding which not only imparts elegance to the edifice, but ensures its durability as well.

The following description of the horizontal brackets is not [illegible] out of place here.

The greatest care must always be taken in fixing the brackets, otherwise the giving way of the whole range may be feared. First of all it is necessary to ascertain that the wall-plates are very firmly compacted. The brackets should then be attached to the small [illegible] hooks which are fixed into the wall-plate.

by means of melted lead poured down into its holes. The spaces between the brackets should then be filled with masonry. There are many other ways of fixing the brackets. Sometimes they are fixed by means of *panjalees* or wooden frames specially intended for the purpose. Others again are secured in the hollows left in course of construction in the walls; and when the wall is dry and stones have been placed over the holes, the brackets are fixed in the hollows, which should be closed with lime and pieces of stone thrust tightly into them. This method of fixing brackets is only useful in a country where roofs are covered by slabs; and the architect's choice of the different methods in vogue can well be guided by observation.

Jhojhas chhujja.—The best way of constructing these is by first fixing the stones of the *chhujjas* into the hollows of the wall left for the purpose in the course of construction, and by thrusting the stone pieces tightly into them when the wall is dry. This mode of constructing *chhujjas* is for the most part applicable when plaster is applied. But when stone facing is used, stone *gurdanas* are built in the wall, the flags of the *chhujja* over such *gurdanas* being let into the masonry. These flags should be supported by props on the scaffolding, which should not be removed until the parapet is finished and the whole thing is dry.

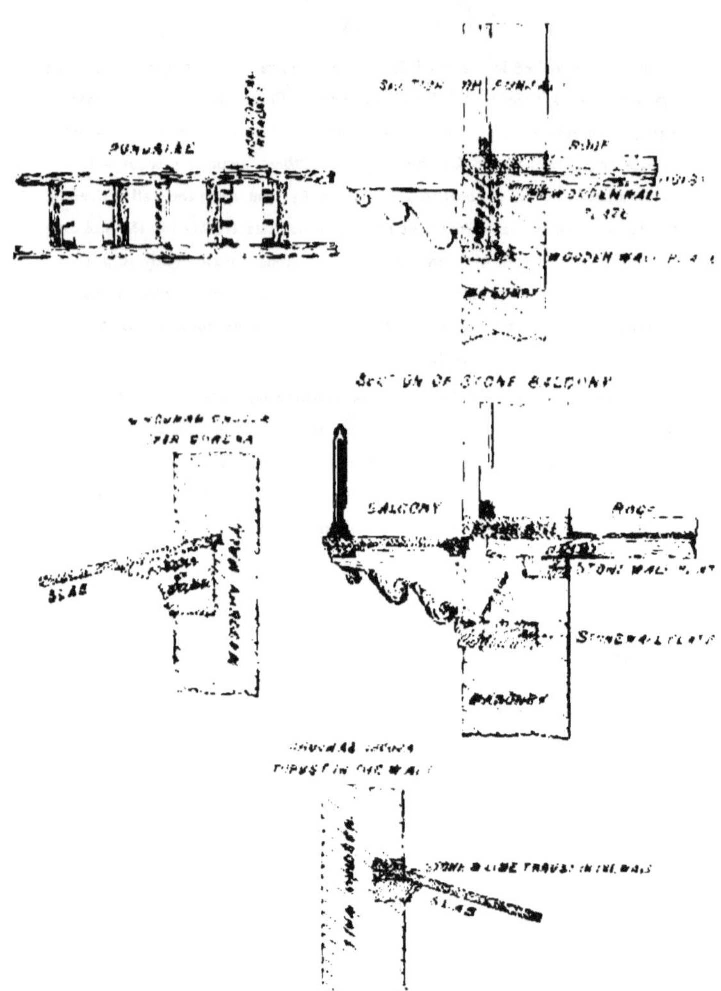

BALCONY
MASONRY
SLAB

PLATE VIII.

The Nalkidar Chhatri.

This *chhatri* is also called Rajashahi. It is especially of Hindu style. It has 4 *jhoomkis* on 4 corners, oval domes on its *pashani*, and a large dome in the centre. In the middle opening, it is usual to erect a *sidra* with tracery decorations. But as this makes it look very heavy, the *shimer gola* arch is fitted in its place, with the view of making it lighter in appearance, and also that much space may not be left between the *pashani* and the opening. The *shimer gola* arch is generally preferred when the opening is intended to be greater in height than what it is in breadth. Railings are always erected on all its four sides, but as the beauty of the columns and *ijara* would have been hidden, they are omitted in the plate. In erecting *shah nashins* Indian potentates also much prefer this kind of facade. Works of this style are generally found at Delhi, Agra, Jeypore, and Ulwar. The one in the Balabhgurh palace, near Delhi, is as good a specimen as any others. A *chhatri* of this kind is erected near the Maharaja of Ulwar's tank at the back of his court. *Marwaris* are made in the *khakandas* of the *jhoomkis* above the *kangoras*. *Marwaris* derive their name from Marwar, where they were invented, and where they are found in ancient buildings. The temple of the Maharaja Ajaipal, at Ajmere, erected long before Mahomedan rule existed in India, has its dome entirely filled with them. The length and breadth of this *chhatri*, being square, is 42 *bux* each, but the proportions of the *shimer gola* arch do not correspond to those given in Plate II. Its *aleens* are 10 *bux* in height. The total height of the *shimer gola* is 18 *bux*, and its breadth 14 *bux*; the breadth of the arch in each corner is 7 *bux*; the height of the *nalki* from the floor to the *kangoras* is 24½ *bux*; the dome 32½ *bux*; the height of the ends to the *gurdanas* of the *chhujjas* 17 *bux*; to the *kangoras* 21 *bux*, and to the *jhoomkis* 29 *bux*. The height of the large dome from the floor is 46 *bux*, and that of the *kursi* 7½ *bux*. The proportion from the projection to the height of the *chhujja* should be in the ratio of 3 to 1.

PLATE IX.

The Sikhar-dar Mandar.

The design of this plate is taken from the Mankamishwar Temple at Agra, though recently built, it is a copy of [illegible] Hindu temples. Its plinth [illegible] has complete adornment. Its [illegible] square but conical dome has around its surface a series of small domes of the same shape, arranged in [illegible] and [illegible] the spectator. An imitation of the sun is placed at the top of the pinnacle or *kalash*. Its chhajja is not of the same proportions given in previous plates, because it is here constructed in lieu of a cornice. This design is generally used for temples, but Anglo-Indians are using them nowadays in ordinary buildings; for instance, both sides of the principal entrance to the Mayo College at Ajmere are adorned with small [illegible] conical domes.

PLATE X.

The Samadh.

Consisting of [illegible] different styles taken from [illegible] different buildings, this design has been adopted for the Maharaja of Ulwar's railway station. It belongs to the Hindu order of architecture, and is [illegible] resemble [illegible] building of the Rajputana [illegible]. Its [illegible] are [illegible] *chhajjas* [illegible] *chhajjas*, and [illegible] *pakhams*. Being [illegible] its [illegible] can be said to be a square building [illegible] length [illegible] its breadth should be [illegible]. Its *kangura* are crowned with [illegible] of flying leaves. The [illegible] are [illegible] lengthwise [illegible] would [illegible] [illegible]. The centre opening has been constructed a little higher than the other openings on the two sides in order to cover the space caused by the [illegible] of the *pakhams*. Were this not so, the space between the *pakhams* and the [illegible] would have been too [illegible] and open. [illegible] *belas* or tracery were used in accordance with present fashion, the building would have a heavy appearance. The advantage gained by making the middle opening higher than the other two openings is that an [illegible] ness may be imparted to the whole structure. Its dome is oval because the length of the *bungla* is greater than its breadth. The pendants generally made in its inner corners are described in detail in the explanations appended to Plate XX.

Construction.

Kursi or plinth	3½	*bux.*
Height of pillar	10	*bux.*
Height from floor to *pashani*	18	*bux.*
" " " to *gurdana*	20¾	*bux.*
" " " to *senga*	14½	*bux.*
Total height	28½	*bux.*
Length of *bungla*	27	*bux.*
Breadth of central opening	6	*bux.*
" of side opening	5	*bux.*

PLATE XI.

The Pointed Dome.

Fig. 1. *The Khasdan-ki Chhatri.*—As its name implies this *chhatri* or dome is of the *khasdan* type. Its *kangoras* are made in the form of a crown, and the dome is gracefully raised to a point above it. Its *jhojhao chhujjas* are undulating. I have never met with similar *chhujjas* except in the temple of Baba Nanuk at Amritsur, and there these undulating decorations largely contribute to the elegance of the structure. On the three centres of the undulated *jhojhao chujja* in each face of the *chhatri* pinacles or kuluss are made. The Dasa is covered with floral ornamentation either carved in stone or made in plaster.

Construction.

Height of *aleen*	9	*bux.*
" of opening	16	*bux.*
Breadth of opening	9½	*bux.*

These proportions differ somewhat from those given in Plate X. Like the *bungla* it has two *pashans*. The height of the *chhajja* from the floor is [illegible], to the dome it is 24⅞ [illegible] and from the *dasa* to the crown 24⅞ [illegible], but by a mistake this is given in the plate as [illegible]. Its corners, though projecting, are equal to the thickness of the walls. *Nage* are made on the corners.

Fig. 2. This *chhatri*, [illegible] dome, was first used in the reign of Jehangir. The [illegible] of *chhajjas* employed in this [illegible] differ in its proportions from those given in Plate [illegible]. The reason assigned for this is that the brackets [illegible] projecting, and [illegible] at the present [illegible] they give more shade. [illegible] that these *chhatris* [illegible]. They are not only [illegible], but they are useful [illegible] the purposes of [illegible]. The [illegible] brackets are made [illegible] the columns as if they were [illegible] to each other, and [illegible] by the [illegible], and the [illegible] are subsequently [illegible]. The columns are of the time of Jehangir.

Dimensions.*

The [illegible] of the *chhatri* [illegible] pillar [illegible]	1[illegible]	[illegible]
[illegible] of pillar		[illegible]
Height to [illegible]	1[illegible]	[illegible]
" parapet	2[illegible]	[illegible]
" [illegible]	2[illegible]	[illegible]

Fig. 3. *The Sidara*.—This is generally [illegible] the *Barahdari*, so called because the three openings [illegible] of the four [illegible] twelve openings. [illegible] the centre opening [illegible] made larger than the two other openings [illegible] flying [illegible] the [illegible] would have been [illegible] with the other [illegible] attached. [illegible]

The centre opening in this plate is 4½ *bux* and the side openings are 3½ *bux*. It is apparent that the difference in the height of both openings in Plate I. is due to the length being obstructed by the work above. Had the openings in this plate been in accordance with the proportions given in Plate I., the *chhujjas* and flying leaves on the top would not have looked well. The height of the column is 9 *bux*, and the height of the centre opening is 17 *bux*. The whole *sidara* being square, its height and breadth are equal or 21 *bux* each. If the drawing were made in accordance with the proportions set for the *sidara* in Plate I., the height would have increased greatly, and the edifice would have had an awkward appearance. This kind of *sidara* is made when it is desired to increase the height of the building. The addition of flying leaves increases the height, and gives it the appearance of a crown.

PLATE XII.

The Husht Pahloo Chhatri.

This octagonal *chhatri* is generally built by the Hindus for their temples in honour of Mahadeo. It has eight openings; and as it is often found in Mahomedan buildings, it may be considered to be of composite style. In Mahomedan buildings its columns are similar to those given in Plate III., and are of Mahomedan style. The work inside the dome is represented in Plate XXV., Fig. 2. This work is also Indian, and in Mahomedan buildings the *galibs* are like those given in Plate XXIV. *Galibs* are of several sorts, but this specimen is one of the best. The proportions of the breadth of its openings are less than those given in Plate I., this being due to the octagonal form of the *chhatri*. The breadth of the openings over these columns looks small. Reduced columns would not be appropriate to the *chhatri*, and increased openings would make the *chhatri* heavier. On this account it has been proportioned thus:— Breadth of *chhatri*, 17 *bux*: breadth of opening, 5½ *bux*; height, 12½ *bux*; height reaching to *chhujjas* up to the *gurdanas*, 15½ *bux*; and to the parapet, 19½ *bux*; the whole height up to the dome, 30½ *bux*. The proportions of the *chhujja* are the same as given in the other plates.

PLATE XIII.

The Shahnashin in Hungia.

These *shahnashins* are generally made in walls at the height of 1½ feet or more from the floor, a portion of the thickness of the wall being taken for the purpose. Its lower portion [illegible] which [illegible] is called the *masnad* or seat. Its *chhajja* are [illegible] or leaning, and the dome is [illegible]. It belongs to the Hindu order of architecture, the style of the arch being that known as *Feelpaya*. Similar *shahnashins* will be found in other places also, but the difference in the proportions given here is due to the increase of projection. The depth of the *hungia* depends upon the projection and thickness of the wall; however it can be computed according to whatever the requirements may be. The plate represents a *shahnashin* with only one opening, but those with three openings have greater value on the score of beauty and elegance (see Plate VIII). Its shape will be gathered from the [illegible] *chhajja* described in Plate VIII. The seating arrangements in such *shahnashins* is private, and made in such a way as not to mar their appearance or cause any inconvenience in their use. *Shahnashins* like these, but having three openings are found in the Mahal of [illegible] palace near Delhi, the inner seats of which are made broad and long, thus contributing greatly to the ease and comfort of the sitters. They not only give additional splendour to the buildings in which they are applied, but establish the reputation of their creators as skilful artisans. Their [illegible] should be constructed open, otherwise [illegible] on at such a place in the wall as will not spoil the beauty of the edifice. When rooms are made in tiers, either for decorative or for more useful purposes, the principal room is constructed in this style.

Construction.

Height of plinth .... [illegible] feet.

" of opening .... [illegible] feet.

Breadth of opening .... [illegible] feet.

Total height .... [illegible] feet.

PLATE XIV.

Oriel Window.

This window was adopted for the Canning College at Lucknow, and much resembles English oriel windows. When I visited Rajputana I found that this description of window was by no means a new thing, for I met with a good many works in this style. Similar windows are not prevalent at Agra or Delhi, but are very numerous in Ajmere and Jeypore. It will appear from its plan that it is the half of an octagon. The pedestal is made for its support. Above it in each corner two *aleens* are raised in an octagonal shell, affording many advantages. In addition to the elegance these give to the building, they are the best conveyers of light; and this light, coming from a distance, is faint as if obtained through a verandah. Then, in the inner room, at the height of 1½ feet, it forms a very suitable seat, and furnishes a good view of all without. In the upper story it forms a similar seat for taking the air in the hot months. Its dome is a quarter of a sphere, the wall supporting its thrust. From outside it resembles a *phanoos* or lantern, improving the beauty of the *chhatri.* Its height is nearly equal to its breadth, and its depth is equal to half its breadth. Its projection is made with corbelling. The projection together with the wall is 8½ *bux.* The breadth is 17 *bux.* The height of the pedestal is 6¼ *bux.* The height of the window to the parapet 17½ *bux*, and the whole height to the dome is 27¾ *bux.* The sill of the window is 12 *bux* from the floor.

PLATE XV.

Niches.

These niches are generally made in the depth of a wall and very frequently in lieu of windows. When not absolutely necessary they are still made for purposes of adornment. They are sometimes utilized for the reception of statues or fountains, and to avoid blank spaces being left. Care should always be taken not to confound the windows with the door, and the corners, &c., should invariably be made in their places and not anywhere in the middle.

To secure elegance in appearance everything must be appropriately placed. The projection of the *moulding* is very little and therefore reduces the height. Leaves are made on the vault of the arch as it is necessary to beautify each top and bottom. It presents the same appearance as a panel.

Construction.

Breadth	[illegible] *Ins.*
Height	14 *Ins.*
Breadth of panel	[illegible] *Ins.*
Height	[illegible] *Ins.*
Height of *moulding*	2[illegible] *Ins.*

PLATE [illegible]

The Vaulted Arch.

This arch is made over an entrance gate or where it is required to [illegible] up the openings of a verandah, and it affords both beauty and protection. A door is fitted to the inner opening which is not shown in the plate, and the vaulted arch is erected on the outer side. At bottom the opening is at right angles, but the upper part is circular to receive the vault of the arch by means of [illegible] at the side where the roundness ceases, tongues are made.

Construction.

Breadth of outer gate	[illegible] *Ins.*
Height of outer gate	22[illegible] *Ins.*
Breadth of inner door	[illegible] *Ins.*
Height of inner door	[illegible] *Ins.*
Tongues	3 *Ins.*
[illegible]	[illegible] *Ins.*
Height of column	[illegible] *Ins.*
Height of base or plinth	[illegible] *Ins.*

PLATE XVII.

Corner Tower for Palaces or Gardens.

These square corner towers are generally erected in the corners of garden and palace compounds. Its plan has been taken from the Jumma Musjid at Delhi, but there is a little difference between the two. Its first story resembles a plinth and the *chhujjas* stand over the *gurdanas* instead of over the bracket. The first story is built as high as the garden wall; and the *baradhari* above it has been surmounted with a dome. This square tower embellishes the blankness of dead garden walls; and, besides being useful in other ways, the *baradhari* makes a good summer-house or watch-tower. The lower story may be utilized as a store-room or godown. Trellis-work or panels should be constructed in the *takya* or low railing, as vacant corners never look nice, and something like a *surahi* should also be made over them.

Construction.

Plinth	1	*bux.*
Breadth of tower..	4½	*bux.*
Height to *gurdanas*	4½	*bux.*
Height of *gurdanas*	3½	*bux.*
Height of *baradhari* to parapet..........................	5	*bux.*
Height of *takya*	¾	*bux.*

The proportions of the *chhujja* and its slope are the same as given in preceding plates. The pillars are the same as described in Plate III. If the *baradhari* were made of red stone and the dome of white or coloured marble, it would very much improve the appearance.

PLATE XVIII.

Octagonal Corner Tower.

This kind of octagonal corner tower is intended to improve the appearance of the corners of palaces, and is employed in structures of more than one story. It will be seen from the plate that its outward portion has been made into something like verandahs which are adjoining the real verandah, and which have been called *grham-garaksha* of the sentinel's pacing-room. *Thakan-dar, gherenda,* and *dasa* are first made in the plinth, horizontal courses are next given, and the *chhajjas* are designed with the view of affording opportunities for taking the air.

The First Story.—In each side of the octagon of the first story a *makara* or opening, with all its requirements, as described in other places, is made. In every opening the *chhajjas* are placed over the brackets fixed on the *dasa*, and protected by *takea* or railings, from the *pachanis* of the first story have been constructed. These *chhajjas* may be used as summer-seats.

The Second Story.—This is made in accordance with the first story, and any others, if required, should be added in like manner. The *chhajja* of the second story, supported by brackets and surmounting the *phorsat chhajja*, at so much height furnish an elegant appearance to the tower. An octagonal *chhatri* or dome, as described in Plate XII., serving as a crown to the whole structure, stands over the highest story, adding to its beauty and proving useful in other ways. Spiral staircases are often made in such towers, and the *chhatri* above a landing to the staircase as well as serves as a protection from the inclemencies of the weather. Similar towers are erected at the corners of the river frontage of the Taj Mahal at Agra.

PLATE XIX.

The middle figure in this plate is of the Hindu style of architecture, but the other two belong to the Mahomedan style. [illegible] octagons, and the bases and [illegible] the [illegible] of *kumbha* already described in Plate I. [illegible] gonal, but each of its eight sides is rounded off outwards. On the points where two sides meet a triangular bund is made, and a small *chatri* called a *guldasta* is erected on the top with the *bunds* fixed in its *dandees* or shafting, with a dome shaped like a garlic and a pinnacle above it. Bunds are generally in the place where the cornice of a house comes in. The column on the right is also octagonal, and is termed *nurgis*. Its *bunds* on the top correspond with the cornice of the whole edifice, and stand over the *pashani*. Two-thirds of the *surahi* come between the *kangoras*, the rest jutting out above, and resembling a pinnacle. It is usual to leave the top of the middle figure squared without any superstructure.

PLATE XX.

This plate represents a Mahomedan corner pillar found at Qutab, near Delhi, erected over the tomb of the Emperor Altamsh, and is octagonal also. In its middle and at its ends it has square *bunds* which look very elegant. *Pilas* or panels are made on every side. In its construction 1 *bux* should be allowed for its thickness and 17½ *bux* for its height. But these proportions are not absolute, as the height may be increased as much as is desired. The base and capital are of a style which existed anterior to Mahomedan rule.

The Pedestal.— This is generally placed under the base of the pillar, and comes of use in cases where the *paya* is to be heightened. This pedestal is very useful for the adornment of rooms. It becomes very often necessary that the *payas* should be raised higher. The advantage gained by this arrangement is that it prevents the *kursi* or base from being hidden by men standing round it or sitting on the seat, a circumstance that detracts from the beauty of its appearance. Sometimes these pedestals are ornamented with sitting lions or other statues; at other times they are left bare, and then they afford sitting accommodation for individuals who may visit the gardens in which they are erected. Ornamental flower pots and vases for the reception of plants are not unfrequently placed on them.

PLATE XX

[illegible]

[illegible]

[illegible]

PLATE XXII.

Panels.

Panels or *dilas* are essential to beauty, and are used to avoid the deformities caused by blank and dead walls. They are generally made in plinths, openings, roofs, *payas*, and jambs. All masons carve these in stone with decorations in the shape of flowers and leaves or undulations (*bels*), but they are often as skilfully made in brick-work; however, they do not look so well in the latter as they do in stone or plaster. Panels are sunk, raised, or made level with the surface of the wall. There is no limit in the variety of them. Specimens of three kinds are given in Plate X., and of two others in Plate XVI.

PLATE XXIII.

The Taziadar Gumbuz.

This kind of dome is Mahomedan in style. Its *payas* and *aleens* are ordinary khumbas, but its side openings are somewhat narrow. The *pashani* in the centre is like that of the Bungla Dome, and its *kulush* and dome resemble those of a *tazia*. Its dome is a hyperbola. *Mojputtas* or flying leaves of the kind employed in the Bungla are used for decorative purposes. Its *chhujjas* are *jhojhao*, and the balcony is placed upon *gurdanas* instead of brackets. Such *gurdanas* are made with corbelling with the ordinary *takya* over it. This kind of dome is erected upon towers and *boorjs* or corner tower, and is, generally, preferred by Mahomedans. Its proportions in *bux* are given in the plate. Such *chhatris*, like *baradaris*, are erected over square edifices.

PLATE XXIV.

[illegible]

These are largely used by Ma[illegible] in the decoration of the ceiling of [illegible] domes. [illegible] and the plate shows the method [illegible] A [illegible] of the dome. [illegible] of the [illegible] the [illegible] of each [illegible] the [illegible] horizontal [illegible] It should be [illegible] observed [illegible] sometimes the [illegible] being [illegible] and sometimes less. The [illegible] waving lines radiating [illegible] reaching [illegible] the [illegible]. These [illegible] form [illegible] quadrilateral figures which whatever material [illegible] may [illegible] either stone or plaster, [illegible] of [illegible] enough [illegible] waving lines may [illegible] is the case [illegible] which [illegible] the whole [illegible] preserves the [illegible] as cut with several [illegible] the [illegible].

PLATE XXV.

[illegible]

[illegible] a [illegible] stone [illegible]

Figure [illegible] of the [illegible] Ha[illegible] A[illegible] [illegible] of the dome is ornamented with lotus flowers. This temple was built before the Mahomedan era, which proves that the Hindoos were not familiar with arch-work in ancient times.

Figure 2 represents the roof of a temple at Delhi and is very plain, its decorations consisting of simple streaks. This kind of roof is mostly always made for temples on account of its producing a good echo.

Figure 3 is a flat roof found engraved in stone in the abovementioned temple at Ajmere, and consists entirely of chain work and *marwaris.*

The decorations shown in Figure 4 are what is known as *bundrumi jal* or network, bordered with tracery. This kind of network is generally made on wood and is commonly used in many of the buildings at Delhi. The term *rumi* signifies "of or belonging to *Room,*" the Hindustani name for Constantinople, whence it was brought to the East by the Mahomedans. It may be painted in various styles. There is no lack of different kinds of Hindustani roofings, some of which are neat, while many can lay claim to be ranked with what is elegant.

PLATE XXVI.

Floors.

A few specimens of floors are given in this plate. These floors are often formed of stones of various colours.

Figure 1 is called *chhewans* or hexagonal.

Figure 2 is called *jowa phool,* from its being an imitation of the blossoms of a kind of grain.

Figure 3 is also called *jowa phool,* but it will be observed that the pattern of the blossoms is different from the foregoing.

Figure 4 is called *kishteedar*, or boat-shaped.

Figure 5 is called *chowphoolia*, or four-flowered.

Figure 6 is called *phool chhewans*, or having flowers in the shape of a hexagon.

The manner of their construction is detailed together with that of *jalis* or lattices in Plate XXVIII. Various other kinds of [illegible] are made in India equally attractive in appearance. These patterns are sometimes inlaid in stone and sometimes stones and tiles are cut out in their shapes and fixed together in good lime mortar.

PLATE XXXII.

Kanguras.

Kanguras are also of various styles. Five specimens are given in the plate, from which it will be easy to form a general idea of what they are like. Figure 1 represents a *kangura* of the Hindu style, and is made by dividing the proposed height into three equal parts by drawing three equidistant lines at a distance [illegible] of one supposed [illegible] from each other. Like in the *kangurdar* neck, *kanguras* should be erected in the upper portion. Corresponding *kanguras* should be similarly sunk in the opposite or lower portion. Care should be taken to make the curves of upright *kanguras* [illegible] exactly like the curves of downward *kanguras* as is given in the specimen.

Figure 2 contains two Muhammadan specimens. These are made almost in the same way as the specimen in Figure 1. The upper portion of one is prepared in the same manner as Figure 1, the lower portion, however, being different. Its height is [illegible] and the [illegible] *kanguras* [illegible].

Figure 3 delineates [illegible] and [illegible] Muhammadan and Hindu [illegible] [illegible] it is [illegible] easy to [illegible] the height of the design might be given. [illegible] the Hindus [illegible] the pattern of [illegible] found in ancient [illegible] buildings [illegible] the preceding [illegible].

Figure 4 [illegible] ancient buildings [illegible]. Its height is [illegible] divided into [illegible] parts [illegible] the breadth of the [illegible] divided into six parts, each of these parts being equal to each of the parts into which the height is divided. The *kungora* itself takes up the space occupied by five of these parts of the breadth, the remaining part out of the six being left for the intervals on either side of each *kungora*.

In Figure 5 we have a very simple but none the less choice specimen of parapet design found in the royal buildings of Agra and Delhi. Such a pattern is generally adopted for fortresses, the apertures being used as loopholes for musketry.

PLATE XXVIII.

Lattice Work.

The art of making lattice work ranks with the most skilful professions of India. The plate gives six different kinds of lattice work, which may be made in various ways, three of these being noticed below.

(1) *Inlaid Work.*—Inlaid work in which stones of different colours are used, when well finished, rivals the handiwork of Nature itself. Leaves and flowers are very skilfully imitated and elaborated by the process of inlaying, the best specimens extant being afforded by the Taj Mahal and Sikandra at Agra.

(2) *Stone Work.*—Lattices carved in stone or marble are works of the greatest dexterity, betraying great skill on the part of the carvers.

(3) *Plaster Work.*—Where stones cannot conveniently be had, lattices are frequently cut in plaster. This method will now be detailed:—

First build up the place where the trellis or lattice work is to be made with a thin wall of rubble masonry or brick and lime, in order that it may serve as a temporary backing. When no longer required, this may be removed. The lime should be obtained from good limestone and should be kept slacked for upwards of half an hour. It is next passed through a sieve and rendered quite free from all lumps. One-third fine sand is now added to the lime and the whole quantity is well mixed together, very little water being added to the mixture.

A clear space is then levelled off on the ground and the mortar is spread evenly on in a layer [illegible] inches thick, and as soon as it acquires a consistency sufficiently strong to bear the impression of the finger, the mass should be divided by the trowel into small bricks, sized not more than 9 × 4½ inches. A larger size than this would probably cause the core of the brick.

A thin brick wall is then built up in front of the temporary backing mentioned above, and a small quantity of the same mortar, composed of one of lime and four parts of sand, is used for cementing these bricks together. The wall surface being carefully levelled by means of floats and straight edges, is then allowed to dry for about a day.

On the next day the pattern required is drawn on it by means of compasses and a string powdered with charcoal. If an elaborate pattern is required, it is first drawn on paper and then pricked through. The paper is then placed on the surface of the wall, and on powdered charcoal being scattered over it the required pattern is left on the wall. The hollow spaces are then neatly cut out with the pointed trowels and chisels, water being gently sprinkled on the work every now and then to keep it moist.

The pattern is cut right through to the backing, which is removed in two or three days, or as soon as the lattice is sufficiently dry to stand by itself. The work may be coloured in whatever tint is desired, and if it should be desired to polish the lattice, this can be done by applying a thin coat of pure lime and powdered marble well mixed and sifted, and polished after a day or so with the same instruments used before. When it is properly polished, it presents the appearance of pure marble, and will last for many years.

Mode of delineation of lattice work designs.—In order that the student may obtain some knowledge of their mode of delineation, linear drawings of some of the specimens given in Plate XXVIII, and the two succeeding plates are here given.

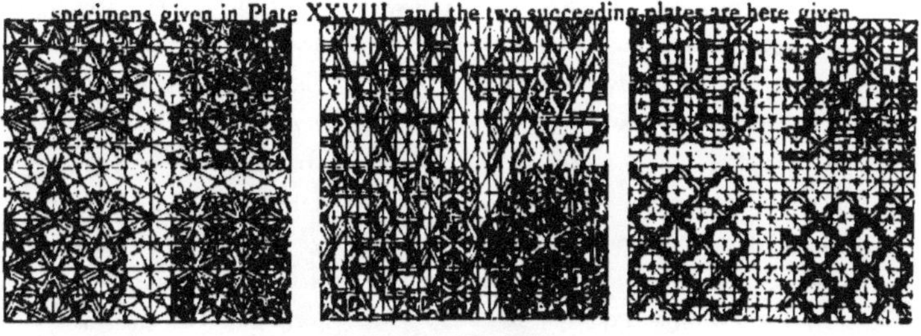

PLATE XXIX.

Lattice Work.

Six other specimens of lattice work are furnished in this plate, respectively called—

Phunda Chhewans.

Mukra.

Gaz Athwans.

Chokee Athwans.

Bindhee Athwans.

Kooza Bundroom.

PLATE XXX.

Lattice Work.

This plate also contains six other specimens of *jali* or lattice work, *viz.*—

Khurpa Benti.

Malund.

Gol Phool.

Dholuck.

Seepra Sada.

Luhurya.

PLATE XXXI.

Maharaja Ulwar's Station.

This is the frontage of the private railway station of His Highness the Maharaja of Ulwar, and is situated about a mile from that city. The buildings consist of a station and other rooms and miscellaneous buildings, and the style of architecture throughout is [illegible] Hindu style. It consists of a central hall and two rooms with a covered platform for His Highness's carriage. The details of the design have been taken from some of the best known and most admired types and forms of important and pleasing structures. It consists of a central entrance hall, leading from which there are two retiring rooms for ladies, and on the other side the same accommodation for gentlemen. The front of the building is shaded by a broad and handsome verandah, while at the back there is a covered platform and line of rails connected with the other station, [illegible] that the carriage of His Highness or any member of the family can be quickly reached. The courtyards on either side of the building are walled for this purpose also. The whole of the [illegible]. This plate is only given to enable the student to see for himself how all the different portions of the edifice, including [illegible], are harmoniously [illegible] put together. The [illegible] of white marble and [illegible] stone [illegible]. The middle portion of the building is projected forward for the carriage, and [illegible] containing a [illegible]. The [illegible] is what is called Bangla-dar, and the [illegible] on the two wings is [illegible]. Over all these openings [illegible] very effectively. *Kungaras* are used on the parapet, with each corner a small *chhatri* or [illegible], as in Plate X, [illegible] the centre of the building, the [illegible] giving [illegible]. The roof is vaulted and adorned with gold, and the inside walls of the rooms are covered with [illegible] decorative work. The whole edifice was built at the expense of the Maharaja, and is the [illegible] of the Indian railways.

PLATE XXXII

Details of Entrance Mahrab

In this plate the details of a Hindustani *mahrab* are given. The *mahrab*, [illegible], [illegible], [illegible], &c., &c., are shown on a large scale. The drawing is taken from an ordinary native dwelling-house at Agra in the locality known as [illegible]. It is cut out in stone, but carved so well as to bear the appearance of having been graved in wax. The work is of the most ordinary Hindustani style, and is found in the houses of people who could not be counted among the wealthy. There are lotus(?) leaves and [illegible] flowers over its [illegible] on the entire arch(?). Its *bangri* and the [illegible] of its [illegible] are decorated with *marori*. Its [illegible] is ornamented with the tree or cypress tree, and its [illegible] [illegible]. In the panels of the [illegible] is tracery work surrounded by *marori*. Its *khambe* differ somewhat from those in Plate I, in having one [illegible] *mathee* in the base, but the [illegible] [illegible] of the usual kind. The capitals, however, are totally different, each being shaped in imitation of the plantain flower. [illegible] [illegible] Its [illegible] is also different, being of the kind specially employed [illegible] the [illegible] [illegible]. [illegible] drawing [illegible] made [illegible] [illegible] Hindustani [illegible] being [illegible] Mahomedan period by Hindu architects.

GLOSSARY.

[illegible]—[illegible].

Bali or [illegible]—[illegible].

Baradari—A pavilion with twelve openings, three on each side.

Bindi athpahl—*Bindi*, literally a point. The ornament worn by native women in the middle of the forehead. *Athpahl*, eight-sided. An eight-sided design of lattice work.

[illegible]—Capital.

Burj—Tower.

Bund—Tie.

Bunrumi—Made in the Constantinople or Roum style.

Bunrumi jal (see *Bunrumi*).—A species of network made after a pattern imported from Constantinople or Rome.

Bangla (see *Bungalow*).—A lightly built structure larger than a *chhatri*.

Bungri—Semicircular openings used for decorative purposes in a kind of Hindustani arch.

Bungridar—Made in the shape of *bungris*.

Bungridar mehrab—An arch having bungris.

Bar—A cubit, or unit of measure.

Chhat—The part over the capital of a pillar, used [illegible].

Chhepahl—Six-sided.

Chhap—A kind of Hindustani bracket.

Chauk athpahl—Flowering design inscribed in an eight-sided, used as a pattern for lattice work. The *chauk* is a native female ornament.

Chauki—Base.

Chaupahla—Four-flowered.

Chhajja—Shades.

Chuliya—A sort of *bungri* made over the meeting-point of a *bungridar* arch.

Dandas—Skirting.

Dasa—Wall-plate.

Dhe—Panels.

[illegible]—The [illegible]. A lattice-work design made in the shape of [illegible].

Fringama—from F[illegible]. An European.

Gahli—[illegible].

Gaz Ashtani—*Gaz*, a rod. Rods made into an eight-sided design of lattice-work.

Ghalandar Chhajja—Concrete corbelling under a *chhajja*.

Ghulam gardish—An outside waiting place for servants.

Gol Phool—Round flower. Any kind of decoration shaped like round flowers.

Guldasta—A corner column shaped like a bunch of flowers.

Gulu—The neck. Used to denote the narrowest part of round pillars.

Gurdana—A support for a *chhajja* projecting from a wall.

Gurdana-ki-chhajja—A *chhajja* supported by a *gurdana*.

Hasht Pahlu Chhatri—An octagonal pavilion.

Izara—A skirt. The pattern or set of moulded work used for decorating and keeping clean the lower portion of a wall.

Jalis—Open lattice work.

Jehangirshahi—Of the time of the Emperor Jehangir.

Jehangir Dara—(or *darwaza*). A frontage of three openings of the time of the Emperor Jehangir.

Jhomka—Small domes made [illegible] largely used as a pattern for native female earrings.

[illegible] Chhajja—Sliding shutters.

Jowa Phool—The flower of a kind of grain, used as a design for lattice work.

Kangni—Pendant. A decoration made in an Indian cornice.

Kairi—Decoration shaped like young mangoes.

Kalas—Literally the point of the head. A [illegible] of arch.

Khalandar—Decoration on the bottom portion of a [illegible].

Khasjamate [illegible]—A pavilion shaped like a *Khadim*, or place for [illegible] here.

Khatam-bandi [illegible]—[illegible] and [illegible].

Khamra (or *khambi*)—Pillar.

Khurpa [illegible]—Literally a sickle with a handle. Battlement [illegible] this shape.

Kishtinuma—Boat-shaped.

Kunda-bandi [illegible]—Fastenings shaped like water-jars. A [illegible] work. Derived from Jaina [illegible] and water-jar.

Kalgi—Ornaments made like egret feathers.

Khidki—Windows.

Kangura—Battlement parapet ornaments.

Kangura—[illegible] parapet.

Kuras—Plinth.

Lasa—[illegible] stone.

Lakarna—Bracketing.

Mahal—Palace.

Makbara (also *makbah*)—An arch.

Malund—A plain rectangular pattern for [illegible] work.

Marwari—Decorations originally designed in Marwar, Rajputana.

Mauraia—Decoration in imitation of waving leaves.

Mauchha—Literally a [illegible]. The [illegible] and [illegible].

Mehrab—[illegible].

Makra—A spider. A kind of [illegible] work [illegible] imitation of the spider.

Matka—[illegible] made in [illegible] water-jars.

Nag—Literally a snake. [illegible] serpentine [illegible] a [illegible] arch.

Palki—A kind of open palanquin [illegible] shaped like a *palki*.

Palkinuma chhatri—A [illegible] pavilion shaped like a *palki* or open palanquin.

Pacha—[illegible].

I

Nimak-ki-mandi.—The Salt Market, a locality in Agra.

Nargis.—[illegible] shaped like the flower of the nargis plant.

Panjabbar.—Frames specially made for fixing brackets.

Pata.—Literally the boat. A space left round the interior of an arch which may be filled up with tracery and inscriptions or left blank like panels.

Peshani.—A frontage arch—Literally the forehead.

Patao.—Lintel.

Pawa.—Pillars.

Phasani.—A kind of Muhammadan [illegible].

Phul-ki-khwan.—Bunch of flowers. A kind of lattice work.

Phunda.—The middle portion of the plinth lying between the *kani* and *kasawdar*.

Phunda-khuman.—Inverted semicircular figures, used as a pattern on balustrades.

Phuran.—Grouped together as in the palm of the hand.

Rajpatan.—Literally belonging or pertaining to Rajas. An architecture of Hindu style.

Raula.—Ropework.

Sahnchi.—A small open place in front of a courtyard or sitting room, but still held to the main building.

Sardal.—Lintel.

Seepi-rass.—Plain shells. Lattice work made like plain shells.

Senga.—The meeting point of two rounded arches, so called from its resemblance to a horn.

Shahnashin.—Literally a king's seat. Also used to mean large daises or raised seats.

Shahnashin-ka-bungla.—A pavilion at corners like a king's throne.

Shahtir.—Lintel.

Shamsi gola.—A kind of arch.

Sidara.—A frontage of three openings.

Shikhardar mandir.—A temple with a roof rising like a steeple or cone.

[illegible]—Flawless lime.

Sanduq—Made like a casket or box, rectangular.

[illegible]—Water-pot.

Sare—Decorations in imitation of the cypress tree.

Tak—A niche.

Takya—Literally a cushion for the back. In Hindustani architecture a low railing for resting against.

[illegible]—Literally a [illegible]. The base of a pillar or column.

[illegible]—The lintel over two pillars.

[illegible]—Flower decoration generally made over the *chhajja*.

[illegible]—Pavilions of Muhammadan design.

[illegible] Gumbaz—Domes shaped like [illegible].

[illegible]—Brackets.

Tatti—Protections from wind, sun or rain, over any kind of opening. Also used to mean light walls.

Zanjira—Chainwork.

ERRATA.

Page	Line	Word	Should be
23	23	Jhomk.	Jhomki.
24	16	30	3
25	11	Jhojhas.	Jhojhao.
26	diagram in two places.	ditto.	ditto.
29	13	Kuluss.	Kulush.
32	13	openiings.	openings.
36	2	Kakan.	Khakan.
"	6	mahra.	mahrab.
"	26	Khunba.	Khumba.
38	4 into two places.	storys.	stories.
39	9	specilmens.	specimens.
40	2	Galids.	Galibs.
43	6	pattem.	pattern.
48	4	Baradarce.	Baradaroe.
51	1	mund.	mundi.

TANTA
KATUF
KURSI
GULLA
TAP
2
2
2
2

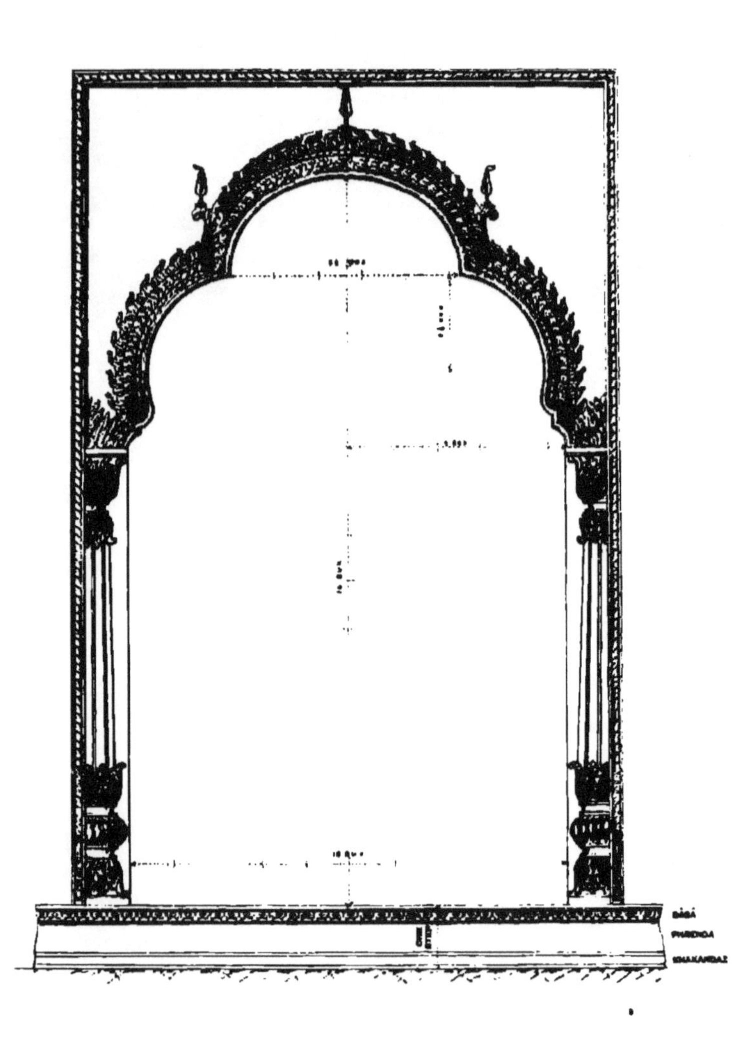

SHIMER GOLA ARCH.

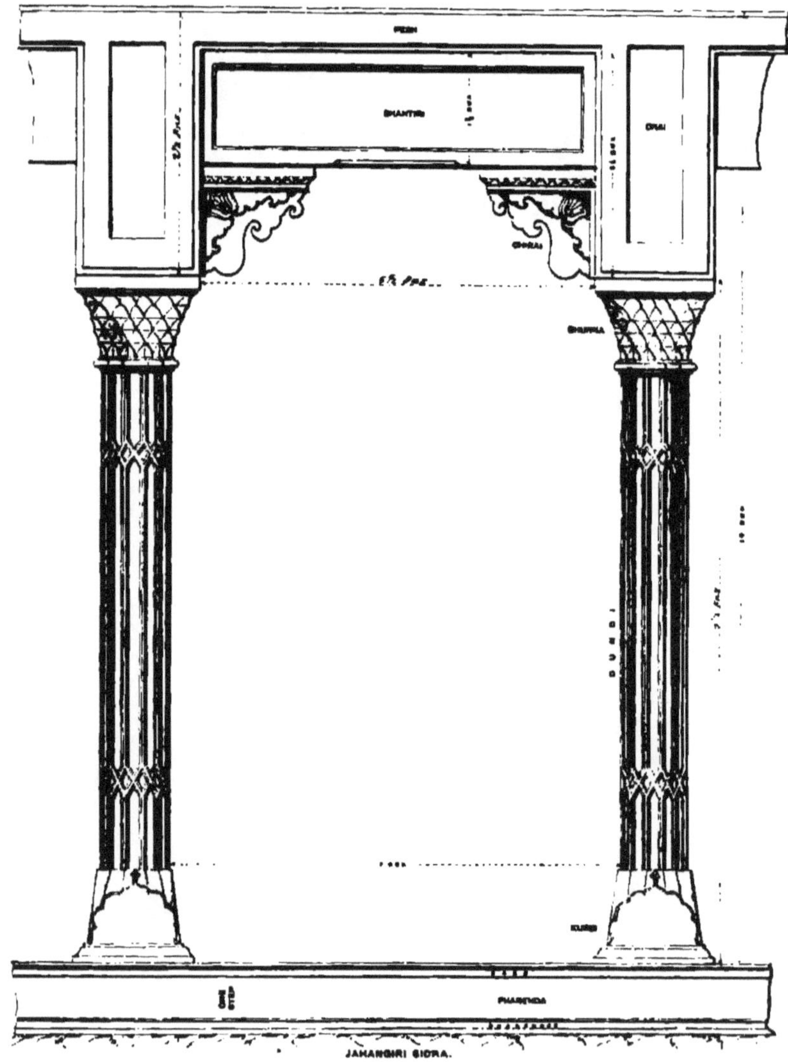

JAHANGIRI SIDRA.

FRINGANA.

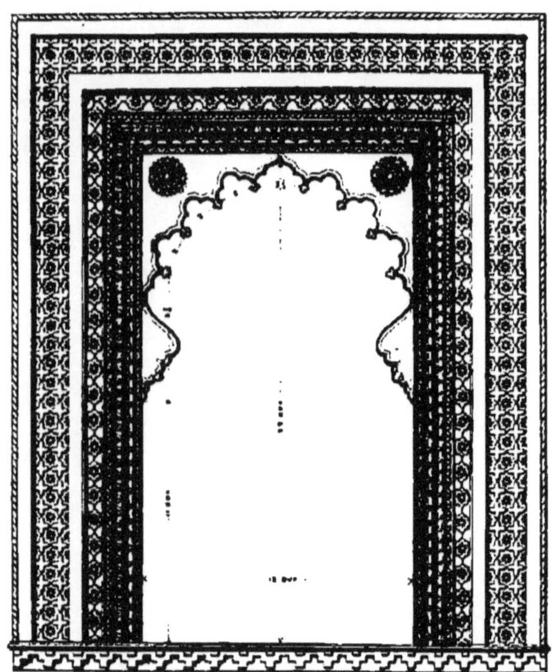

ENTRANCE—TEMPO JAHANGIR.

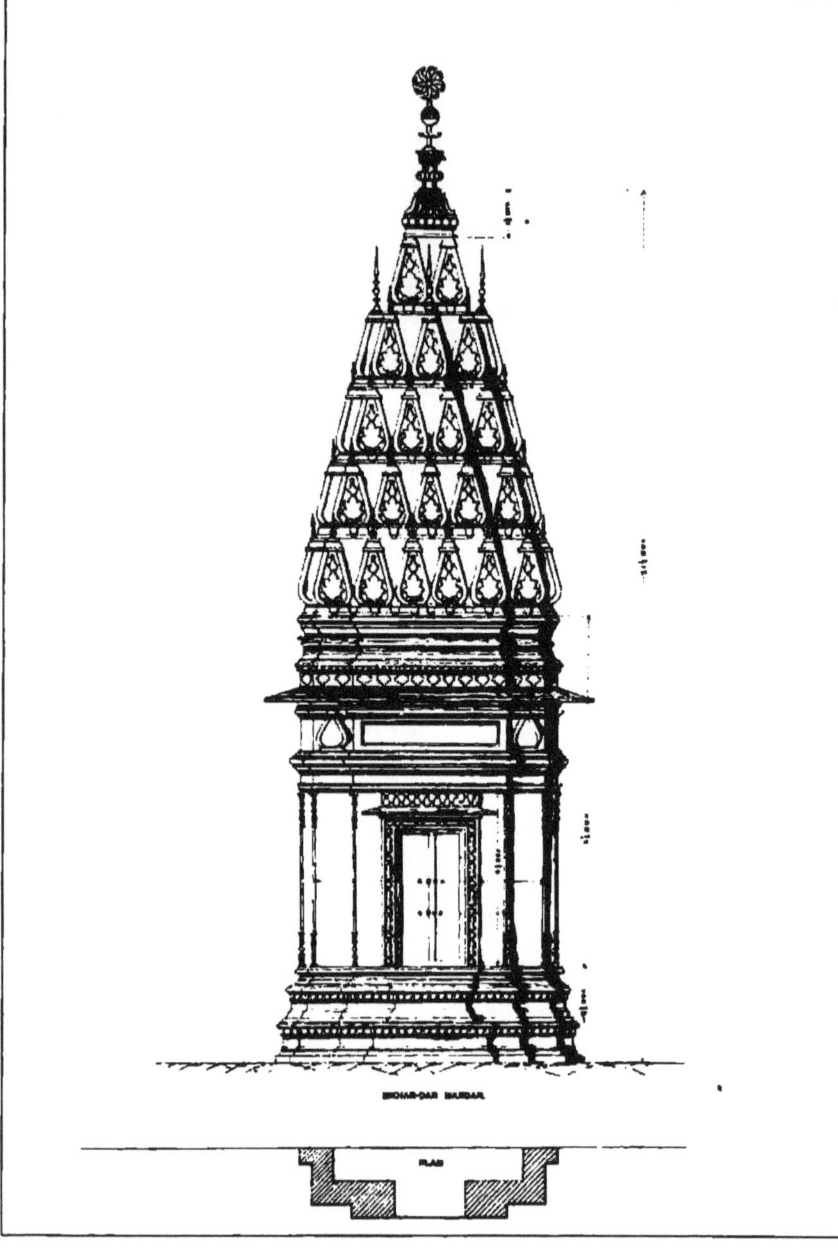

SIKHAR-DAR MANDAR.

PLAN

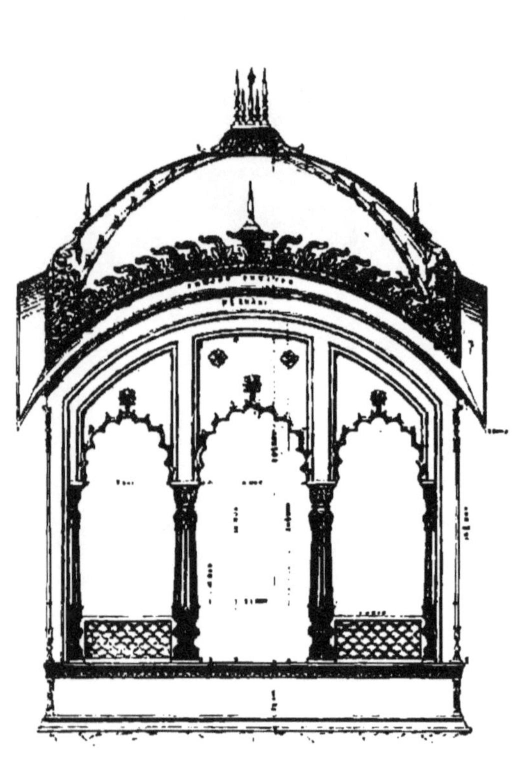

BUNGLA

SIDARA.

KHASDAN-KI CHHATRI.

CHHATRI.

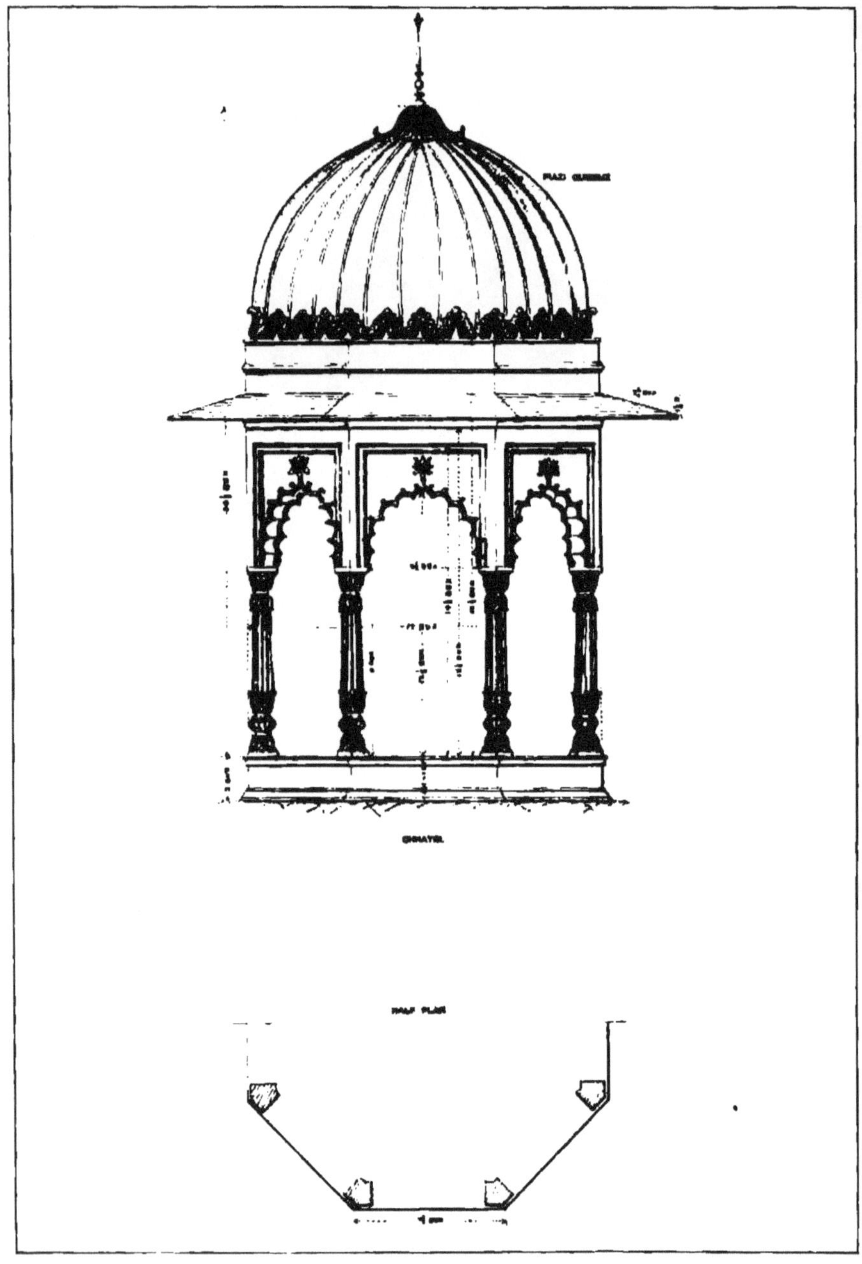

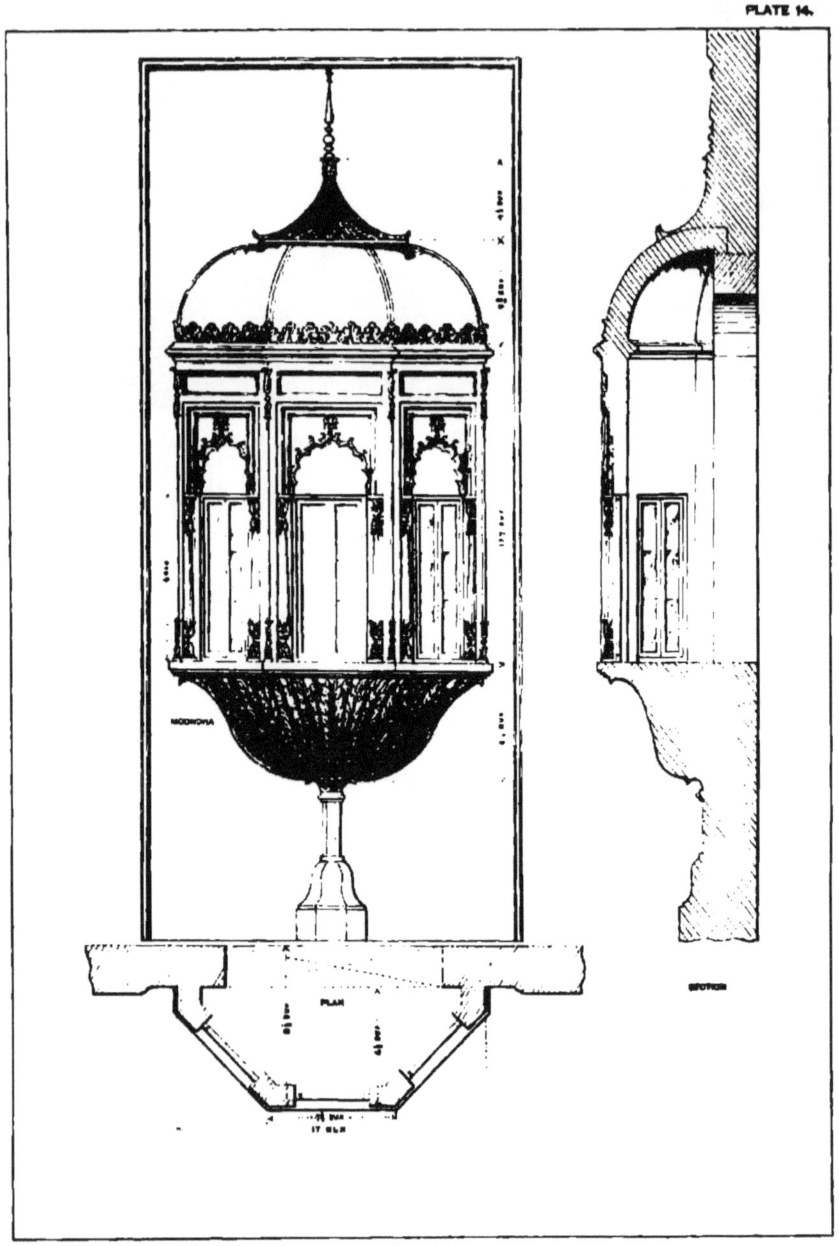

ORIEL WINDOW.

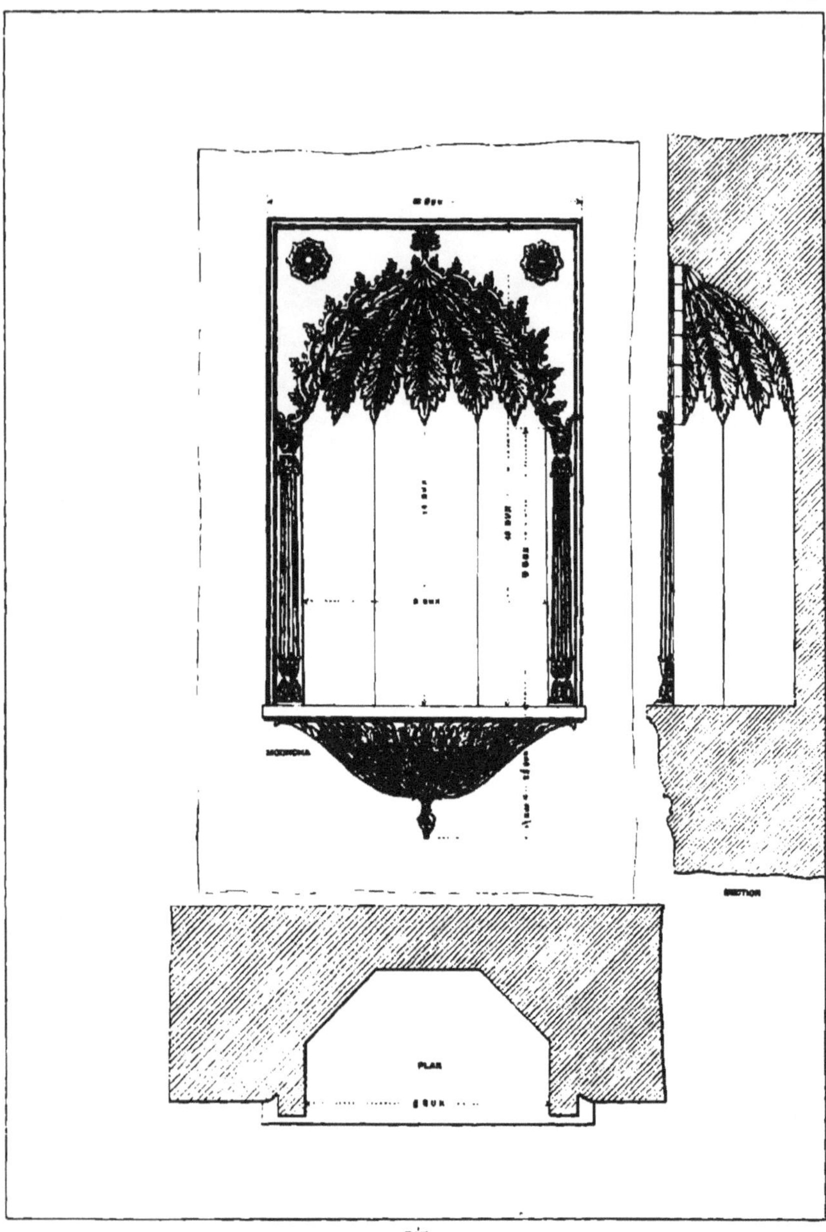

TÁK

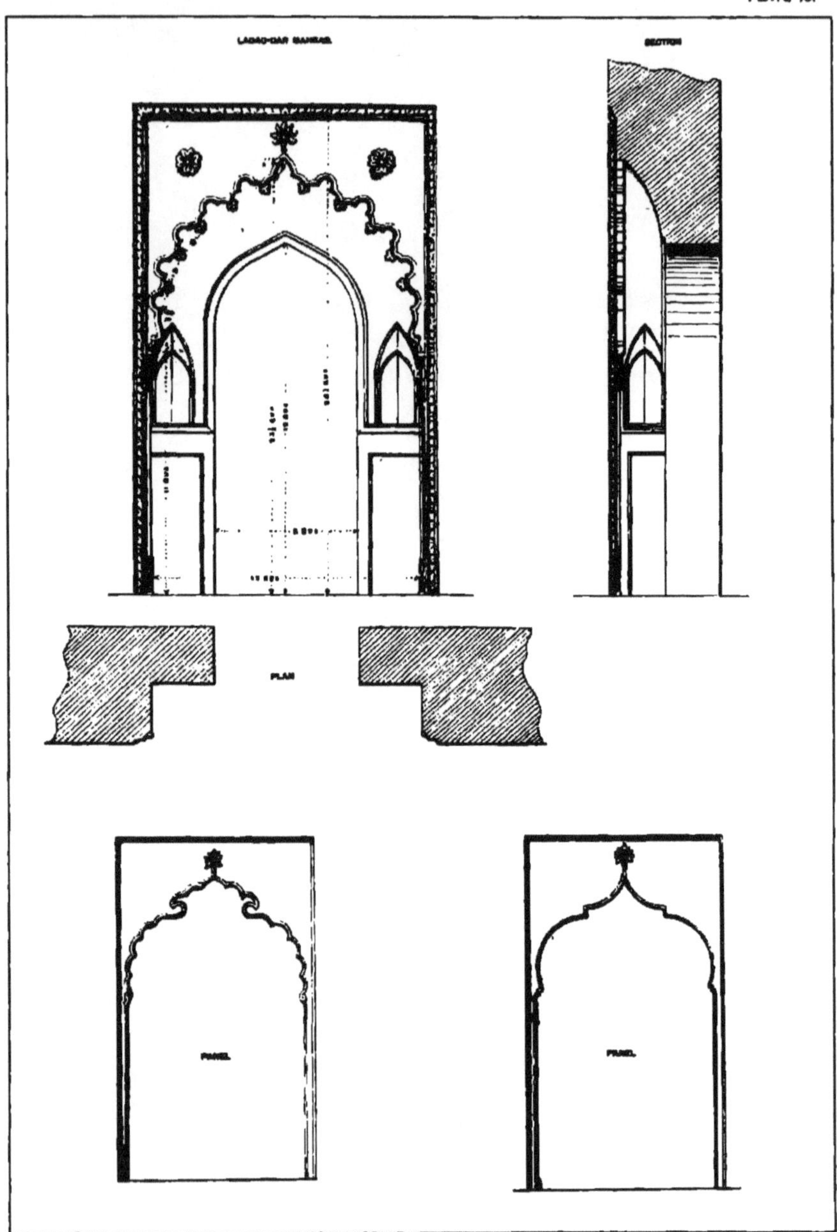
SECTION
PLAN
PANEL
PANEL

PLATE 17.

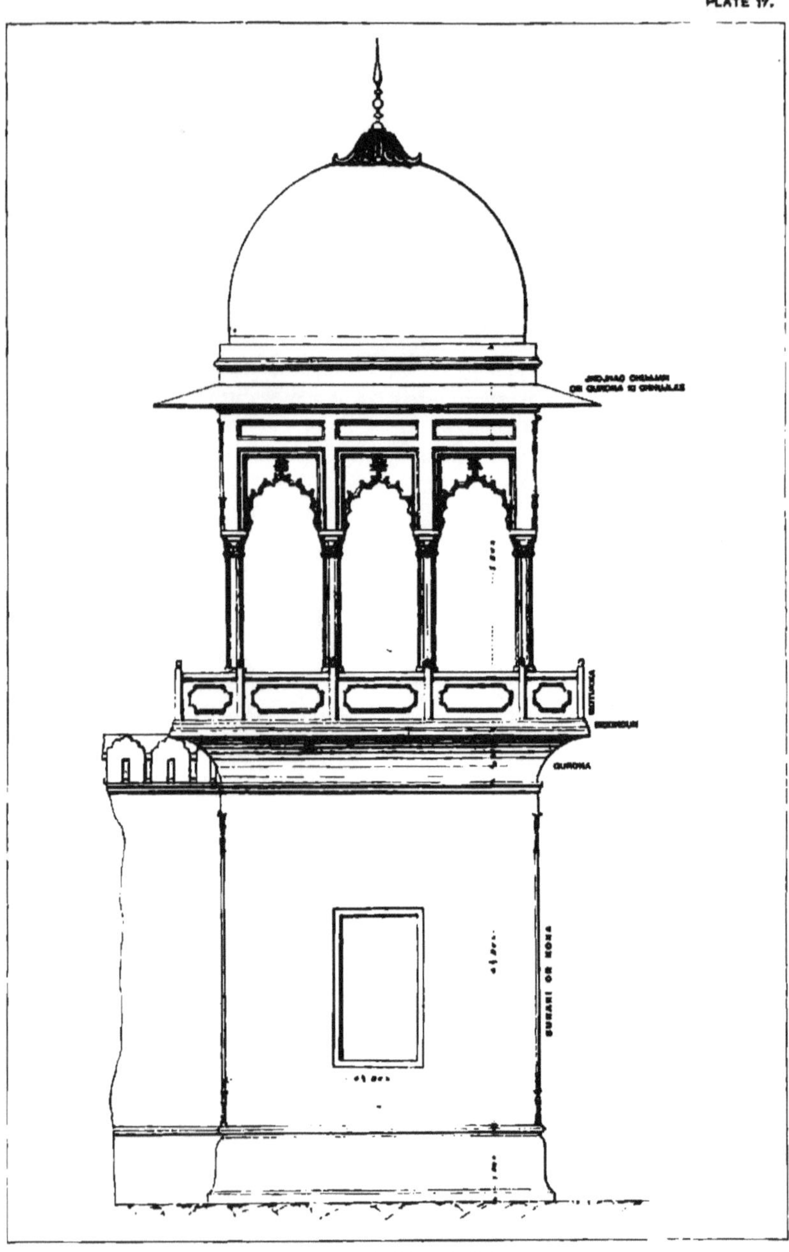

CORNER TOWER FOR PALACES OR GARDENS.

CORNER TOWER.

PLATE 19.

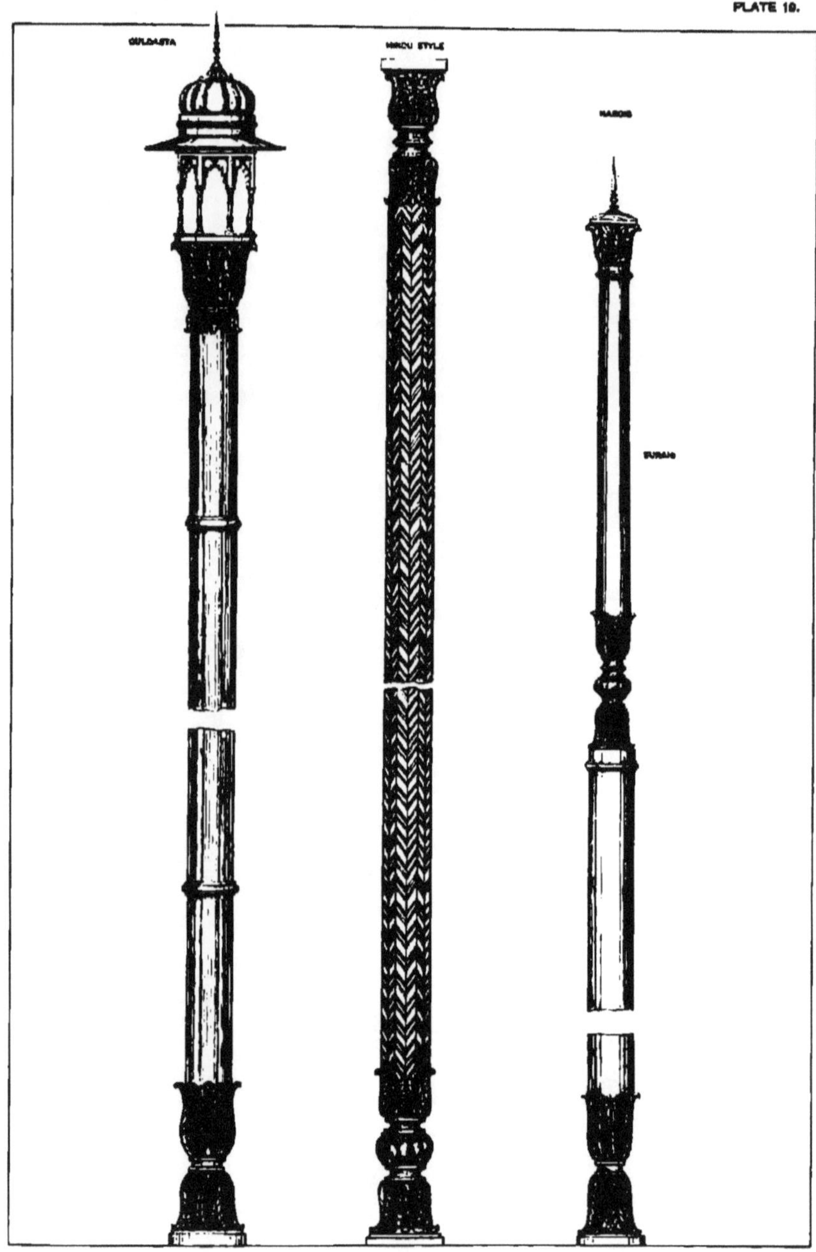

CORNERS.

PLATE 20.

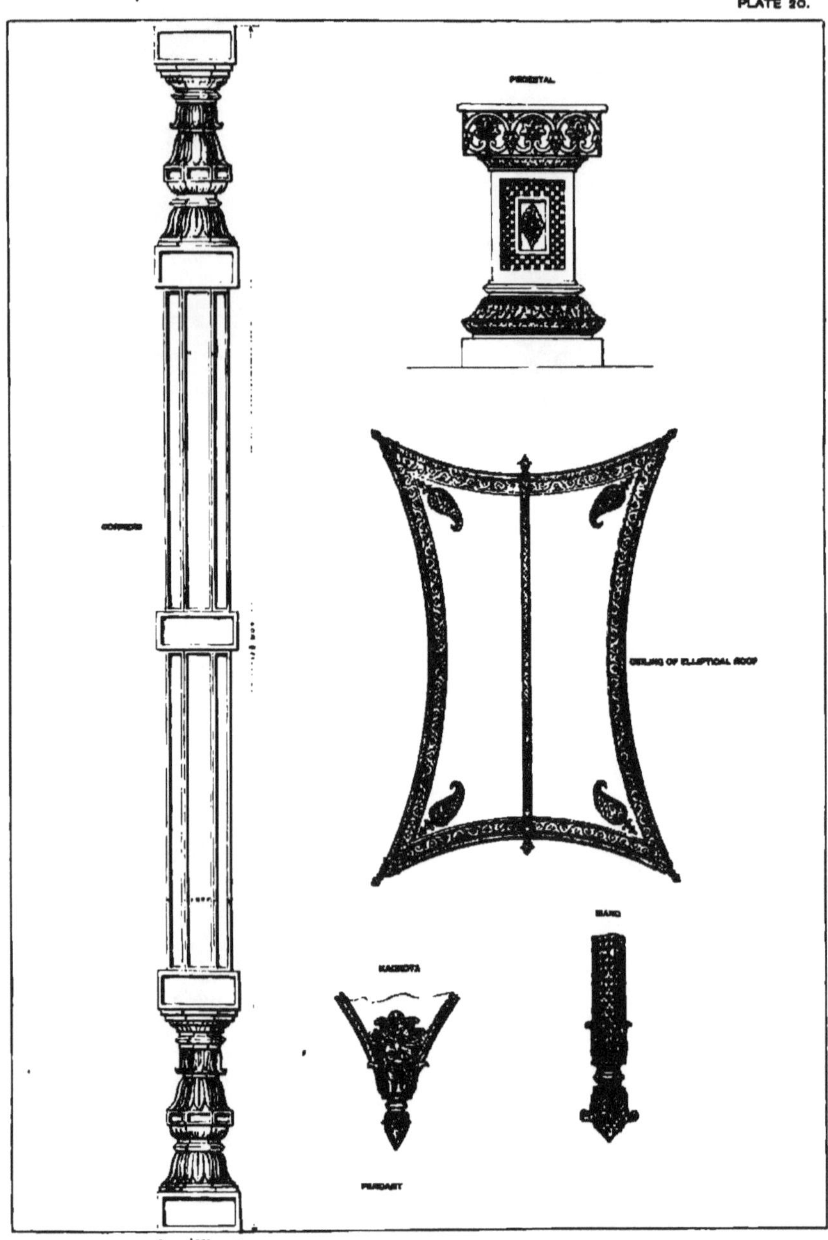

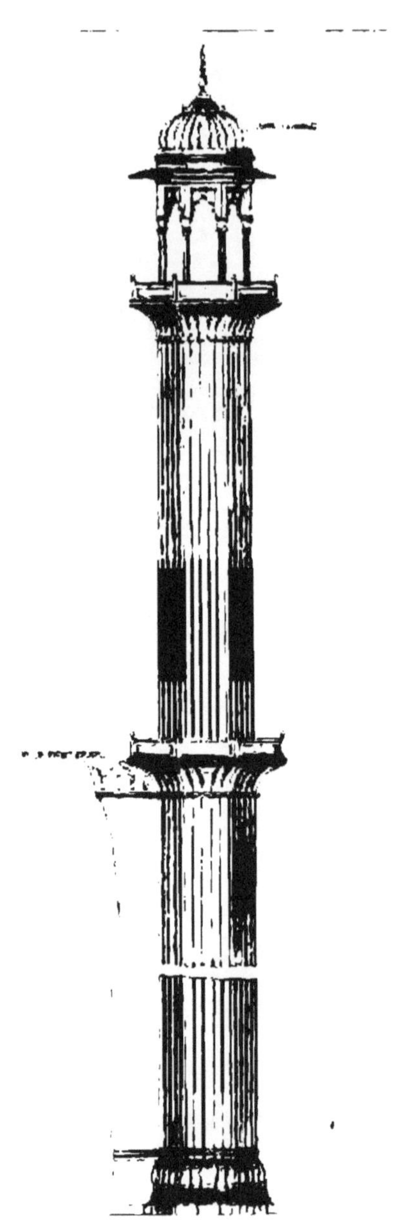

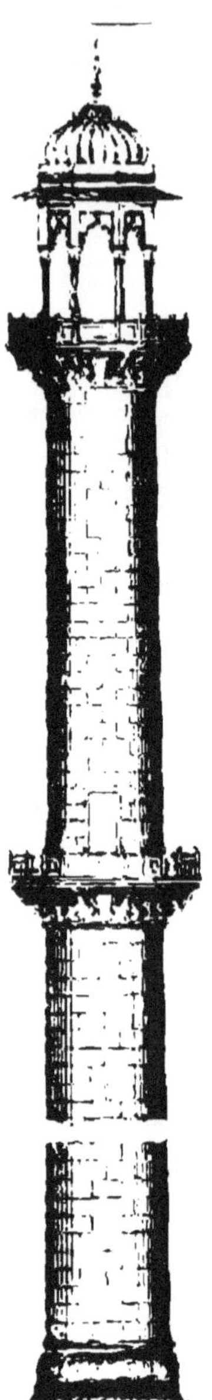

TAZIA-DAR GUMBUZ.

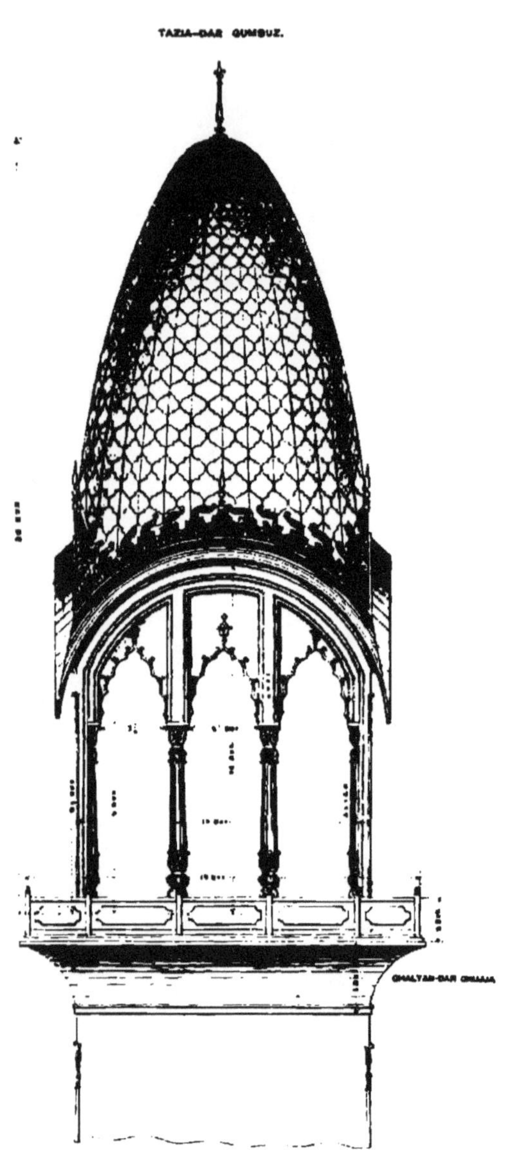

PLATE 24.

FIG. 3
FLAT STONE ROOF

FIG. 4
KHATUN-GUNDI-KI CHHUT

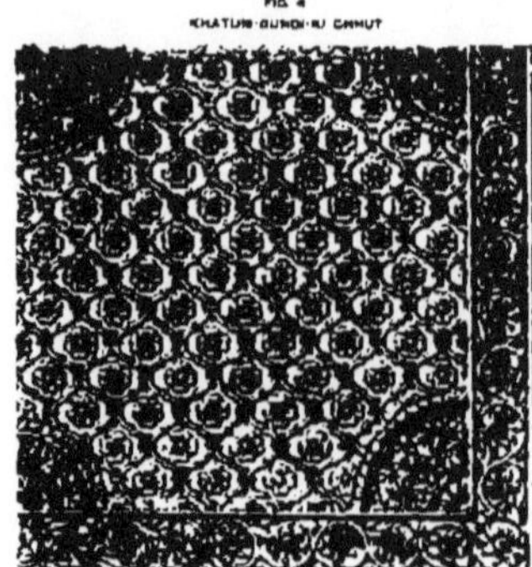

FIG. 2
HEMISPHERICAL DOME

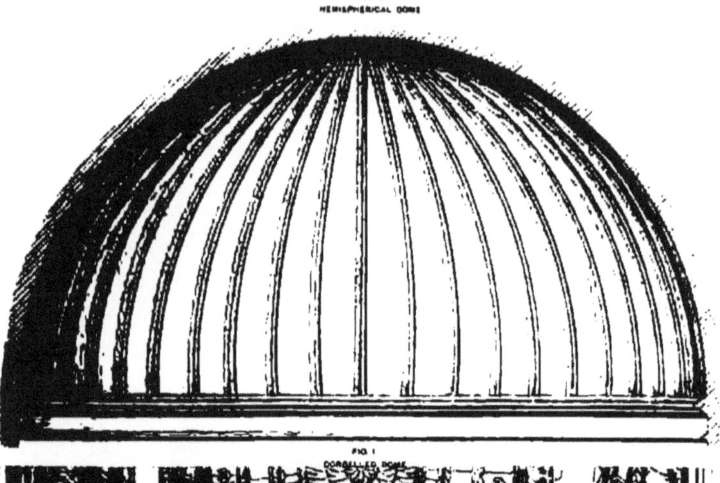

FIG. 1
CORBELLED DOME

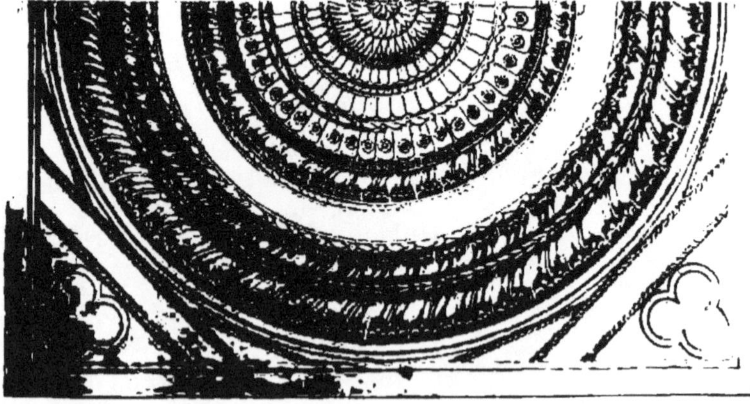

FLOOR.

CHEWANS

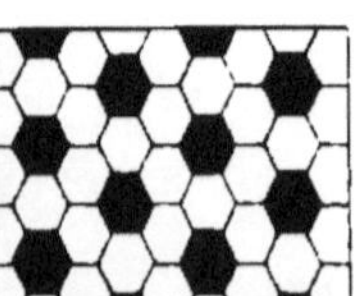

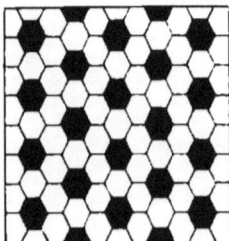

JAWA CHEWANS

JAWA CHO PHOLIA

KISHTEE

CHO PHOLIA

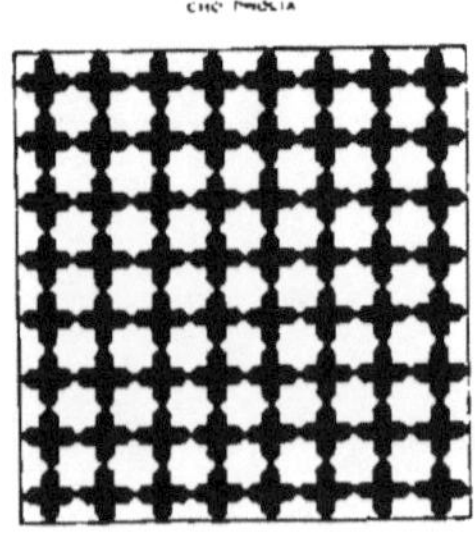

PHOOL CHEWANS

KUNGRA

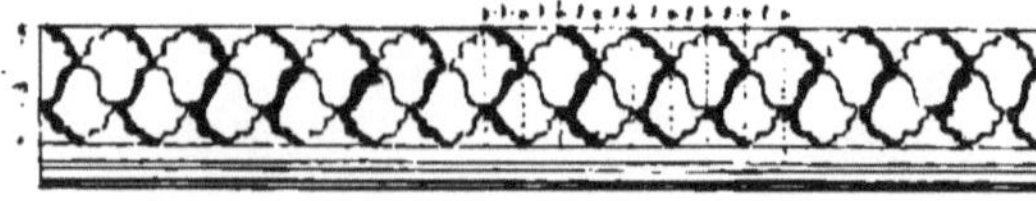

KUNGRA

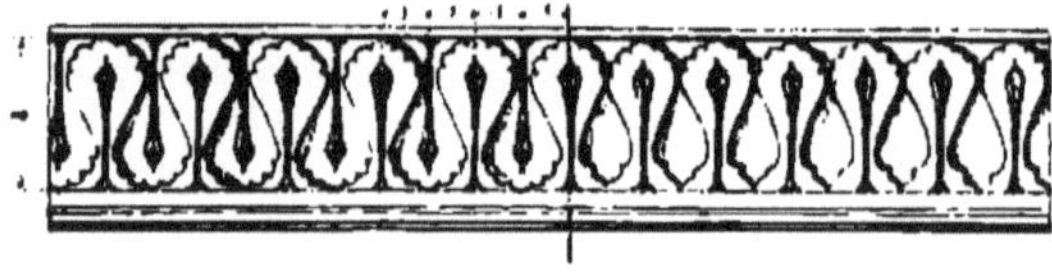

KANGURAY

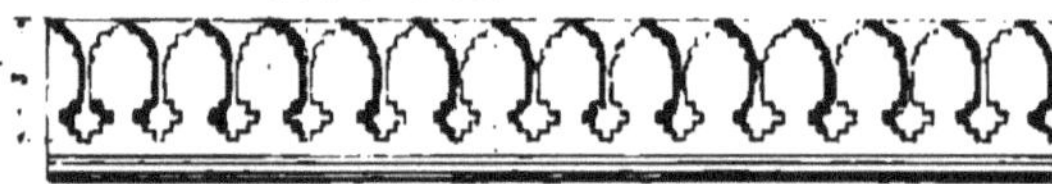

KUNGRA

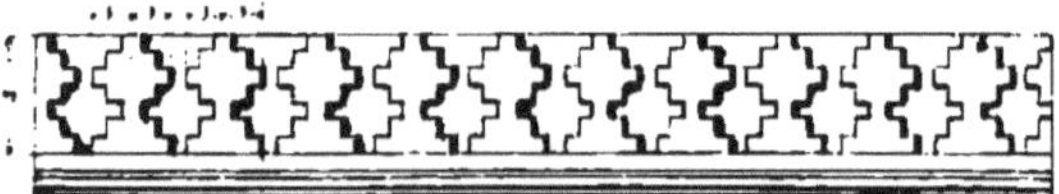

KANGURAY

PARAPETS.

JÁLI WORK.

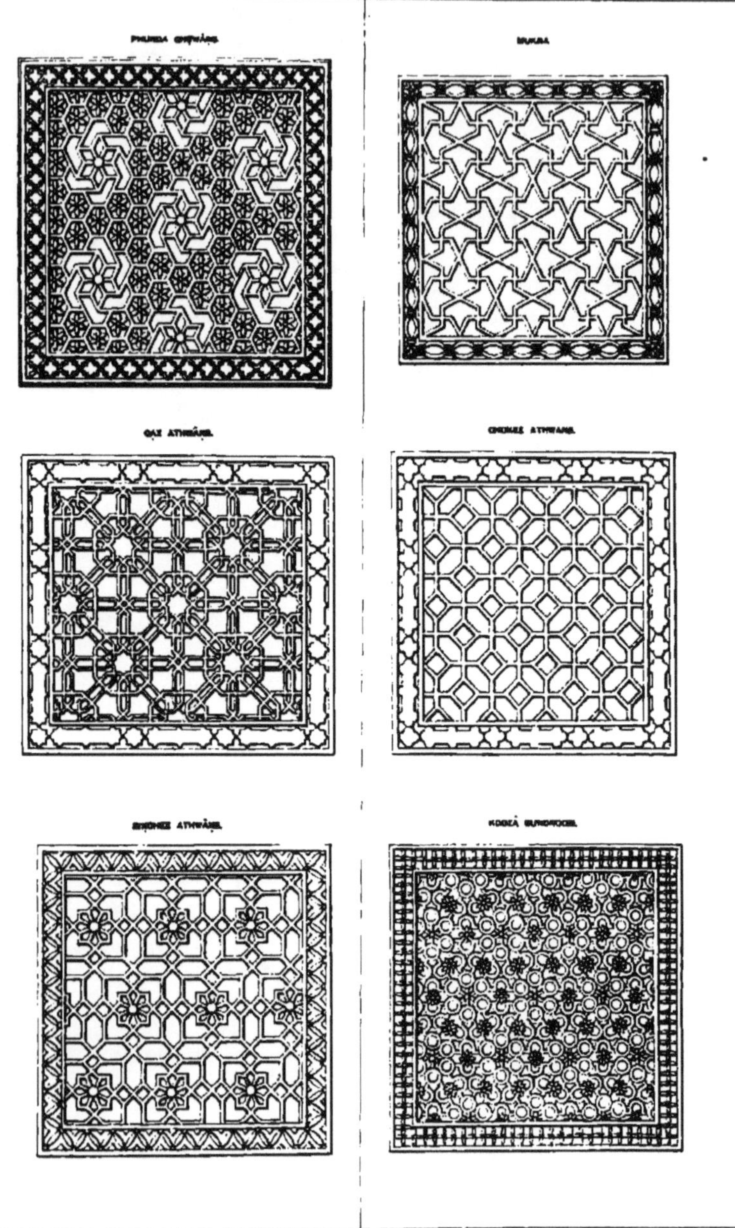

JĀLI WORK.

PLATE 80.

JĀLI WORK.

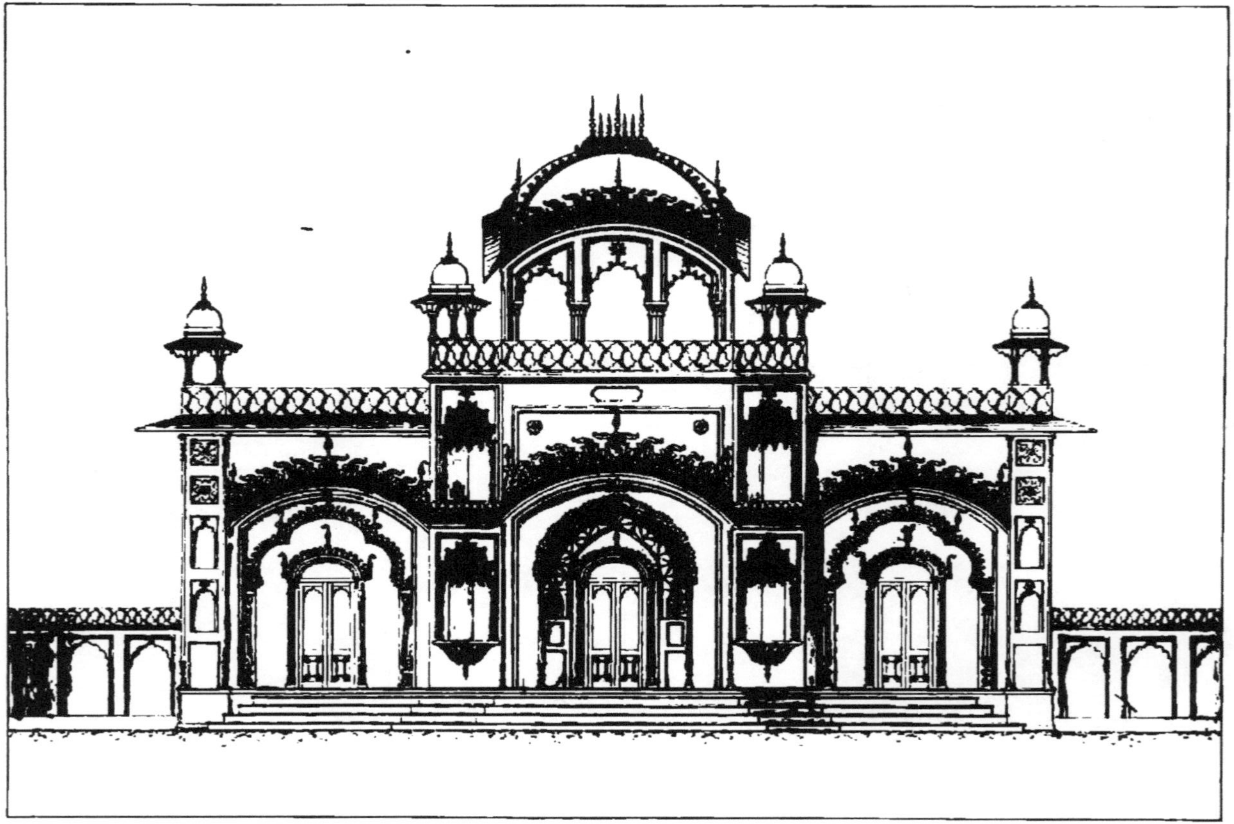

MAHARAJA ULWAR'S STATION.

PLATE 32.

DETAIL OF ENTRANCE. MHRAB.

www.ingramcontent.com/pod-product-compliance
Lightning Source LLC
Chambersburg PA
CBHW030623270326
41927CB00007B/1287

9783337385156